Harry Milles Fenn, Frederick Diodati Thompson, Harry Fenn

In the Track of the Sun

Readings From the Diary of a Globe Trotter

Harry Milles Fenn, Frederick Diodati Thompson, Harry Fenn

In the Track of the Sun
Readings From the Diary of a Globe Trotter

ISBN/EAN: 9783744662857

Printed in Europe, USA, Canada, Australia, Japan

Cover: Foto ©Andreas Hilbeck / pixelio.de

More available books at **www.hansebooks.com**

IN THE TRACK OF THE SUN

READINGS FROM THE DIARY OF A GLOBE TROTTER

BY

FREDERICK DIODATI THOMPSON

WITH MANY ILLUSTRATIONS BY MR. HARRY FENN AND FROM PHOTOGRAPHS

NEW YORK
D. APPLETON AND COMPANY
1893

COPYRIGHT, 1893,
BY D. APPLETON AND COMPANY.

ELECTROTYPED AND PRINTED
AT THE APPLETON PRESS, U. S. A.

TO
HIS IMPERIAL MAJESTY THE SULTAN
ABDUL-HAMID II
THIS VOLUME
IS MOST RESPECTFULLY DEDICATED
BY
THE AUTHOR

The Imambara at Lucknow.

CONTENTS.

	CHAPTER I.	PAGE
NEW YORK TO TACOMA		1
	CHAPTER II.	
VICTORIA TO YOKOHAMA		12
	CHAPTER III.	
IN JAPAN		36
	CHAPTER IV.	
FAREWELL TO JAPAN		52
	CHAPTER V.	
VISIT TO CHINA		65
	CHAPTER VI.	
THROUGH THE STRAITS TO CEYLON		84
	CHAPTER VII.	
IN HINDOSTAN		105

CHAPTER VIII.
Up the Ganges 117

CHAPTER IX.
Agra and Delhi 134

CHAPTER X.
In Western India and Egypt 152

CHAPTER XI.
On the Nile 171

CHAPTER XII.
Visit to Palestine 186

CHAPTER XIII.
Home through Europe 206

CHAPTER XIV.
Familiar Places Revisited 217

LIST OF FULL-PAGE ILLUSTRATIONS.

	FACING PAGE
Statue of Daibutzu, or Great Buddha	*Frontispiece*
An Indian camp	5
British war-ships at Esquimalt, near Victoria, B. C.	15
Japanese wrestlers	27
Pagoda at Ueno	33
Garden at Nikko	38
The sacred bridge at Nikko	41
Koro at Nikko	44
The cave at Enoshima	48
A view of Fusiyama	51
The principal street in Ozaki after the great earthquake	53
A Japanese vender of vegetables	56
Tame deer at Nara	59
A Joss-house, Hong-Kong	66
Foreign buildings on Sha-Mien Island, Canton	69
The five-story pagoda, Canton	71
The race-course in Happy Valley, Hong-Kong	72
Chinese criminals awaiting death	75
After the execution	76
Public garden, Hong-Kong	79
Private residence and grounds, Hong-Kong	81
Queen's Road Central, Hong-Kong	82
A Ceylon elephant	85
The Sultan of Johore's palace, near Singapore	87
A nutmeg plantation, Penang	89
Temple at Penang	90
Native fishing-boats, Colombo	93
A street in Colombo	95
Cabbage palms, Ceylon	97
Mustering of coolies on a tea estate, Ceylon	98
Double bullock-carts, Colombo	100
Entrance to gardens at Pérádeniya, near Colombo	102
The Hall of Horses, Seringham	109
Jain idols conveyed in a bullock cart	113
A snake-charmer	115
Drawing toddy in Bengal	118

LIST OF FULL-PAGE ILLUSTRATIONS.

	FACING PAGE
A Nepaulese Ranee and attendants	121
The highest mountain in the world, viewed from Darjeeling	122
Method of burning the dead on the banks of the Ganges	125
The place containing an impression of Vishnu's feet in stone, at Benares	127
General view of Lucknow from the clock-tower	128
The residency, Lucknow	131
Scene of the attempted escape from the massacre, 1857	136
The Taj Mahal, Agra	140
The Pearl Mosque in fort, Delhi	145
Sun-procession day, Jeypore	148
Colonel Elphinstone and the author on the Maharajah's elephant	154
Entrance to the Caves of Elephanta	158
The railway station, Bombay	160
A Bedouin sheik from the neighbourhood of Ghaza	164
The base of the Great Pyramid	167
The Sphinx	168
A Soudanese warrior	172
A Turkish and an Egyptian woman	175
The Sphinx at Karnak	176
A bride going to her husband, Egypt	179
Tombs of the kings, Thebes	181
The Great Temple at Karnak	183
Obelisks at Karnak	184
Colossal statues of Memnon, Thebes	187
A Mohammedan sheik	188
The Garden of Gethsemane	190
The stone of unction, Jerusalem	192
Interior of the tomb of the Virgin, Jerusalem	194
The rock in the Mosque of Omar	197
A scene on the river Jordan	198
The Mount of Olives	200
The Grotto of the Nativity at Bethlehem, showing the manger	202
View of Jaffa from the house of Simon the Tanner	204
Interior of a Jewish house at Damascus	206
Mohammedans at prayer in the Great Mosque at Damascus	209
General view of the Principality of Monaco	213
General view of Naples	215
General view of Sorrento	216
House of Pansa, Pompeii	219
The Bourse, Paris	220
Interior of St. Peter's, Rome	222
Houses of Parliament, London	225

WITH HEADPIECES, INITIALS, AND NUMEROUS OTHER ILLUSTRATIONS IN THE TEXT.

IN THE TRACK OF THE SUN.

CHAPTER I.

NEW YORK TO TACOMA.

IT was Wednesday, October 14, 1891—a perfect American autumn day—when I boarded the Pennsylvania limited express for Chicago. The record of a night trip in a Pullman car is not at this date wonderful, but it is none the less very satisfactory. Our sleeping-cars are the perfection of comfort, and the serving of meals in a dining-car is a boon, especially as the meals themselves are excellent, and at moderate cost. I had determined that during my travels I would examine critically the railway systems of the countries through which I passed, and note my impressions. I had several hours in Chicago, and amused myself by taking a hansom cab and looking at the city. One is ready to acknowledge that Chicago is a wonderful place, when he considers that

but sixty years ago it was a miasmatic marsh, with a few log cabins for trappers, on what was then called by the pungent name of Skunk Creek. Time has changed all that; and the change, though not so swift as the raising of Aladdin's tower, has its own wonders. In one respect at least it is well that the Columbian Exposition is to be held there, for such a fact as the growth and present status of Chicago cannot fail to impress foreigners with a sense of that stupendous impetus which characterizes the New World, and compels the wonder of those who see its results.

After dinner at the Richelieu Hotel I returned to the railway station and had my luggage checked to Portland, Oregon, a distance of over twenty-three hundred miles. When I awoke, at about eight o'clock the next morning, after another night of comfort, I was crossing the State of Iowa, through a magnificent farming country that everywhere showed signs of abundant production and prosperity.

Independence Hall, Philadelphia.

At Council Bluffs, shunting our sleeper to the Union Pacific train, we crossed the Missouri, and from Omaha continued on our way over lands still fertile and well cultivated. Twenty-four hours later we reached Sherman, the highest point on the Union Pacific Railroad, eighty-two hundred and forty-seven feet above the sea. The Rockies in the distance were covered with snow, and the rarefaction of the air was very perceptible. The character of the country had entirely changed. Signs

Fine Arts Building, Chicago Exposition

of cultivation had vanished; small shanties dotted the ground at long intervals; herds of cattle, a few horses, and occasionally a coyote, were the only living things to be seen. Soon, however, we reached the thriving city of Laramie, the "Gem City," as some call it, of the Rocky Mountains; and here I bought the Daily Boomerang, a typical Western newspaper, with all the latest news of the region, Laramie being the distributing centre of a large mining and ranching district.

The land looked more barren as we proceeded; but, though crops and tillage were lacking, there was excellent coal. At 8 P. M. we arrived at Green River Junction, parted with the San Francisco section of our train, and proceeded over the Oregon Short Line.

On Sunday morning we pulled up at Shoshone. Three Chinamen and a little Chinese woman got aboard, and an Indian and his squaw, the first Indians we met. On my former journeys there were many at the different stations, and numbers of them were constantly found tak-

Gypsies on the Plains

ing free rides on the platforms of the cars, as they are permitted to do by law.

Twenty-five miles from the railroad are the Shoshone Falls, which are reached by the universal Western institution the stage-coach, or by the pleasanter mode of private conveyance, which can be had easily. A good team traverses the distance in three and a half hours. The falls are not seen until the traveller is close upon them, although a few lava mounds are the only objects that break the long stretch of desert. As the carriage wheels sharply round one of these, a cañon twelve hundred feet deep opens suddenly, and we see Snake River, which is reached by winding down a steep roadway. From a cozy and comfortable hotel

a view of the cataract is obtained. The wild and lonely grandeur of the falls and their bed cannot be described. Through eighteen miles of cañon the river rushes in numerous descents. The greatest of these is nine hundred and fifty feet across. Its first leap is eighty-two feet, the next two hundred and ten feet. The region abounds in marvels. Twin Falls, Blue Lake, the Vaulted Dome, Locomotive Cave, Cascade Fall, the Devil's Corral, Bridal Veil, Bridal Train, National Mill-Race Falls, Eagle Rock, and Bell's Island suggest that man has been far less original in supplying names for the wonders lavished upon him than Nature was in bestowing them. The river is crossed by a cable ferry, which is worked by wires under water and overhead.

In our sleeper, for two nights, we had a deputy sheriff from Seattle, with a Russian Jew prisoner in custody. The latter was a villainous-looking fellow, apparently capable of any crime. The sheriff, about thirty years of age, as he told me, was one of the most muscular and powerful men that I have ever seen. During the day the prisoner sat in his seat, with his ankles chained to-

Pillars of Hercules, Columbia River, Oregon.

gether. At night the sheriff handcuffed himself to the prisoner, and they slept together—an agreeable bedfellow, truly! I cannot help wondering why it is that in the pioneer settlements of the present day ruffianism, vulgarity, and defiance of law are found in close company with advancing civilization. Certainly, whatever the causes were for the superiority of early pioneers, the fact is that the Pilgrim Fathers and the Puritans of New England, the Dutch burghers of New Amsterdam, the Quakers of Pennsylvania, and the Cavaliers of Virginia and Carolina, were refined, honest, respectable men, quite different from the cowboys and hoodlums of the nineteenth century.

Monday morning, at half past four, the porter called me to dress, preparatory to leaving the train at The Dalles. It was still dark when, with several other passengers, I went into the Umadilla House at The Dalles, and shortly after breakfast I departed in the stern-wheel steamboat S. D. Baker down Columbia River.

Block House, Cascades, Columbia River, Oregon, where Grant and Sheridan both served as lieutenants in the army

After a sail of fifty miles we reached the Upper Cascades. Leaving the vessel, we were carried around them for six miles on a narrow-gauge railway, after which we resumed our water journey, and steamed down sixty miles of the magnificent river, which grew broader until it looked almost like an inland sea. One of the most beautiful sights is that of Multnomah Fall, which is broken, like the dust-fall of Lauterbrunnen, into a shimmering mass as it tumbles seven hundred and twenty feet into a hillside basin, and then into the Columbia by another leap of one hundred and thirty feet. The most noticeable feature of the picturesque and varying landscape is Cape Horn, whose thousand feet of surface is seamed like the rocks of the Giant's Causeway.

On the Classra kiver.

The high colouring of various hues of red and gray adds greatly to the effect. Of the same peculiar formation are Rooster Rock and the long line of palisades.

At the junction of the Columbia with its great tributary, the Willamette, is a military post, Fort Vancouver. Here we leave the Columbia, and steam up the almost equally beautiful stream on which stands the handsome city of Portland. On a clear day, from Fort Vancouver may be seen the snow-capped mountains St. Helen's, Jefferson, Adams, Hood, and Rainier. The trouble for the transient visitor is that in "rainy Oregon" the days are too often overcast and the clouds rest heavily on the glacial peaks.

Salmon canning is one of the principal industries of this region, and the great factories employ Chinese workmen largely. The salmon-wheels of the Columbia were a curiosity to me. They are large circular frames on pivots, somewhat resembling water-wheels, and are set at a slight angle in the river, near the shore. The bottom of the

Wheel for catching salmon, Columbia River.

wheel is in the stream, and the current turns it so that such fish as happen along are caught between the floats and carried up until they slide down to a central trough and thence to a receptacle on shore. Some of them are on scows, to be moored at various places. It is probably the laziest method of fishing that has ever been invented.

At about 4 P. M. we arrived in Portland, after a most enjoyable day. I drove to The Portland, a new and beautiful house with a handsome glass *porte cochère* and an interior court filled with large palms and banana trees—quite different from the inferior hotel the traveller was obliged to tolerate when I stopped here two years ago.

Boarding the sleeper at 10 P. M., I found myself next morning at six o'clock in Tacoma. Here, again, there is a beautiful and well-kept hotel, The Tacoma. I took the motor car on Tacoma Avenue to Old Town, to see again the curious little St. Peter's Church, with its bell-tower, which was made by utilizing a large tree growing alongside the edifice. I noted on my way the wonderful development that had been wrought in two short years. The whole avenue, on very high land overlooking Commencement Bay, is now a continuous line of beautiful villas, with lovely gardens and green lawns, all well kept, neat, and attractive.

A singular and interesting fact concerning this region is the absence of poisonous reptiles, insects, or plants. The motor, on its way to what is rather comically called the "Old Town," passes a fine family hotel named The Rochester, from the tower of which can be seen nine beautiful snow-capped peaks. The sky is generally clear, and in the purity of the air the distant objects seem near at hand, while at night the great stars hang out with magnificent lustre. Venus throws a reflection on the sound like the young moon of an Eastern night. A curious effect is the change of colour in the water as the tide from the Pacific rises and falls. When the tide is out, the milky streams that flow from the glaciers turn the deep brown-green waves to pale light green. Even at the city's edge the water is so deep that large vessels moor easily. The steep hillsides covered with dwellings, rising street above street, give a striking effect from the water. Mt. Rainier, called by Tacomaites Mt. Tacoma, is wonderful. Its lofty sides have never been scaled by man, and for some reason no satisfactory pictures

St. Peter's Church, Tacoma

of it have been made by the camera. It has the great advantage of being seen from sea-level, so that its whole height is realized. Generally amid mountain scenery the view is obtained from comparatively lofty regions. Mt. Rainier lifts itself from the plain, with no perceptible foot-hills, more than fourteen thousand feet.

Puget Sound abounds in fine harbours, and its island-dotted surface is wonderfully beautiful. The foliage is of great size, luxuriant, and very

Scene on Puget Sound.

green. The timber from its shores is sent to all the Eastern shipyards. In 1860 William H. Seward said, "Sooner or later the world's ship-yards will be located on Puget Sound." It has been computed that a twelve-hundred-ton ship can be built here twenty thousand dollars cheaper than in Bath, Maine.

One thing which I found noticeable after I left the East is the want of "smartness" in the personal appearance and attire of the people. Dusty clothes, unshaven faces, and unblackened boots are the rule.

As wealth increases in these regions, refinement and cultivation will increase likewise. The American is nervous, spirited, and ambitious. After he has subdued Nature and built cities and towns, and gained the first object—money—the next peculiarly American aim, to have "the best that money can buy," will extend to education, and he will doubtless, sooner or later, prize the privilege of the rich, to buy good taste itself, and next to imitate it. Already, in rude beginnings, refinements are asserting themselves. The habit of chewing tobacco has almost disappeared—wonderful to say—in places where formerly the custom was universal. The next generation will probably pay more attention to the elegancies of life, and doubtless disciples of Ward McAllister will spring up to lead the Four Hundred of the future in our Western cities.

Tacoma suffered several years ago from that Western epidemic, a "boom." People rushed in in great numbers, and the value of city lots went up to fabulous figures. Finally, in the parlance of the country, "the boom busted," and these prices collapsed.

The streets of Tacoma are all paved with wooden planks eight inches in thickness and thirty feet long. The entire roadway is thus covered, and also the sidewalks. I have never seen this elsewhere.

Monday evening, after dinner, I took a "Gurney" cab and drove to the steamboat wharf, where I learned that the Olympian, the boat I expected to take, had been detained at Seattle, for the interesting reason that the engineer and a deck-hand had engaged in a fight, which was democratically participated in also by the captain and a custom-house officer. It resulted in the whole party being arrested; hence the boat could not proceed. Another boat was secured to take the passengers to Seattle, and we were then transferred to the Olympian.

Cowboy life.

Japanese art design.

CHAPTER II.

VICTORIA TO YOKOHAMA.

ON Wednesday morning at dawn we steamed into Victoria, British Columbia. Her Majesty's customhouse officer did not bother me to open my luggage, so I drove to the Driard House, where I found I must wait an hour for breakfast. The interval and the breakfast being disposed of, I sallied out to look again at the town. A great difference in this people from that which I had just left was noticeable at once. The tone of Victoria is distinctly English. Of the population of twenty thousand the majority are English-born. I drove to the Government buildings, which, though inexpensive, look appropriate to their use, amid well-kept grounds, with grass and roads in excellent condition.

Thence I went to the Lieutenant-Governor's residence, the present incumbent of that office being the Hon. Hugh Nelson. In approaching the house we flushed a covey of pheasants, an incident reminding one of Old England. We then passed Dunsmuir Castle, an expensive stone structure, saw many beautiful English-looking country seats and cottages, and turning, drove out to Esquimalt—or Squimalt, as it is invariably called—the naval station of the British Pacific squadron. Here is an excellent dry dock, the best on this coast. It is a perfectly landlocked little harbour, with water sufficient for the largest ships. At anchor were the flagship Warspite, the Garnet, and the Pheasant, all under command of Rear-Admiral Hotham.

Returning, I took luncheon at the "Poodle-Dog Restaurant," and an excellent one it was. The proprietor, Louis Marbœuf, is a veritable *cordon bleu*, competent to cook as good a dinner as one can get at Bignon's or the Café Voisin. I was told that he came over to Mexico as *chef* to the unfortunate Maximilian, and after the

Residence of the Commander in ... Victoria, British Columbia.

collapse of the empire drifted to Victoria, where he has ever since remained.

Luncheon over, I took a walk to Beacon Hill Park, which is charmingly situated directly on the strait. While I walked, a lady on horseback approached, probably the wife or daughter of some naval officer, although I did not discover who she was, but a presence of such distinction that it seemed as if she had been suddenly transported from Rotten Row.

The view from the Lieutenant-Governor's residence and that from Beacon Hill Park are not surpassed by any in this country. The line

Empress of India.

of the Olympic Mountains is seen on the horizon, across the Strait of Juan de Fuca, and to the southeast rises in bold relief the snow-capped Mt. Baker. Opportunities for sport in this neighbourhood are unrivalled. Mountain goats, bear, and deer abound, and the fishing is excellent in the sea and in the rivers. In the streets of Victoria one sees many sailors, red-coated marines, and a few of the Dominion Garrison Artillery, one company of which is stationed there.

After dinner I took my departure on the night boat for Vancouver, arriving there at 8.30 A. M. In approaching the shore I saw the Empress of India, the good ship that was to transport me to the Mikado's island

British war-ships at Esquimalt, near Victoria, B. C. Naval Station, Pacific Squadron.

empire. On landing I drove at once to the Hotel Vancouver, a house owned and managed by the Canadian Pacific Railway. It is a fine new brick and stone building, well situated, with a view of the Cascade Mountains and the inlet, and in all respects pleasant and comfortable. The harbour, called Burrard Inlet or Coal Harbour, resembles a lake, so narrow is its entrance, yet large and laden ships can enter without difficulty. Considering that the city—for city it is—has only existed since 1886, its site before that date being a dense forest, it is a remarkable instance of what can be done in a few years. The buildings are substantially constructed, and the character of the inhabitants is excellent. It is certainly a most desirable town for educated Englishmen and Scotchmen to settle in, for the tone of the place is refined and respectable—everything, indeed, that could be desired.

The hotel is about to be doubled in size, the present accommodations being insufficient on account of the increased travel to Japan and China. The temperature is very equable, never too cold nor too warm, the only drawback being the frequent rains. There is plenty of sunshine also, and the climate is remarkably similar to that about the Lakes of Killarney, in Ireland.

Stanley Park, named for the present Governor-General, Lord Stanley of Preston, is on a beautiful point of land between English Bay and Burrard Inlet. There are many Indians in this part of the Dominion, but they are peaceable and friendly, giving no trouble. Here, as in California and Oregon, cent pieces are never seen, the smallest coin used being the half dime or nickel.

I spent three days at Vancouver, after which my luggage was sent on board the steamer, and I prepared to sail for Yokohama, a distance of forty-three hundred miles.

Sunday, October 25th, was a fine sunny day at Vancouver. At exactly a quarter before 2 P.M. one of the officers walked up to the captain and said, "The mails are all aboard, sir." "Cast off!" was the captain's reply, and in a few minutes the new and stanch steamship Empress of India was under way on her fourth voyage to Japan and

China. A sailor fell overboard while we lay at the wharf, but was rescued after considerable difficulty. Out of the harbour, through the narrows, and into Puget Sound we steamed. At about 7 P. M. we stopped at Victoria to take on board more passengers, principally Chinese, and then, pushing out through the Strait of Juan de Fuca, we were ploughing the Pacific Ocean.

Sailing through Puget Sound, we passed a school of whales, spouting away vigourously and disporting themselves in characteristic gambols.

Our ship registered six thousand tons burden, and was commanded by Captain O. P. Marshall, of the Royal Naval Reserve. She was built under admiralty supervision, and is liable to be taken for a cruiser in case of necessity. We therefore carried the blue instead of the red ensign, which merchant ships usually fly.

We had on board seven missionaries, going to their fields of labour; a correspondent of the London

Daily Chronicle, on his way to Pamir and Thibet, to inquire into the Russian advance in that direction; Shenango Mizuno, Secretary of the Japanese House of Commons, who most courteously invited me to be present at the opening of the Diet by the Mikado; Señor J. M. Rascon, the Mexican minister to Japan, and his beautiful wife, both of whom I found most cultivated and intelligent. All told, there were about ninety first-cabin passengers, twenty in the second cabin, and four hundred and thirty-eight in the steerage, the latter all Chinese returning home. Officers and crew were English, but the stokers and stewards were Chinamen.

Our voyage was very tempestuous from the moment we entered the Pacific Ocean, and grew worse and worse. We were unable to go on deck; windows, doors, and hatches were battened down, and the saloon and library were lighted with electric lights during the day as well as at night. The sailors, in accordance with their old-time superstition, ascribed the storm to the presence of the missionaries on board. We made matters worse by taking an extreme northern course, going within sight of the Aleutian Islands, and getting the full sweep of the gale through Bering Sea and afterward directly off the Kamtchatkan coast.

On Sunday, November 1st, we passed the one hundred and eightieth meridian and dropped the next day out of our lives. There was no November 2d for us. We jumped to Tuesday, the 3d, and could say with the Roman emperor that we had lost a day—though not through any fault of our own. There was a sensation of strangeness and hollowness in having the bottom slip out of time in this manner. It was terrible weather, and we should have been thankful to lose an entire voyageful of such days as we underwent. It seemed a practical joke of Father Chronos, or as if Puck had arranged it in his notable girdling of the earth in forty minutes, or as if somebody had succeeded in boring a round hole through eternity and left it in that condition; but we were not grieved. The next week passed slowly. The sea continued rough, and the wind blew a hurricane, but at last we became accustomed to the weather, and the days were not so disagreeable after all.

On Sunday morning, November 8th, when I awoke, the sea was smooth. The sun shone brightly, and the air was warm and balmy. Once on deck, to my delight I found that we were within two miles of a coast, and in the midst of a fleet of perhaps a hundred Japanese fishing-junks. These were the first sails we had seen since leaving Puget Sound, and this was Japan.

The sail up to Yokohama I found most interesting, moving as we did along the shore, and passing innumerable boats of all sizes and shapes, some sailing and others being rowed. At half past twelve we entered the inner harbour, and cast anchor alongside vessels of all nations, principally warships. We were at once surrounded by a swarm of small boats called *sampans*, with one or two oars, if I may so call the implement with which the little craft were propelled, very much in the same manner as are the gondolas at Venice.

All was confusion, each oarsman striving to get his boat nearer than those of the others to the side of the steamer, in hope of securing a job to carry some one ashore. These boatmen frequently wear only a small strip of white cotton cloth just wide enough to prevent total nakedness, and their brown skins look extremely picturesque. The Japanese are serenely free from false modesty. My guide on a later occasion took me into a bathing-house. There were about a dozen women present, all entirely nude, but they paid no attention to our presence, and did not seem in the least degree disconcerted, and they were all perfectly respectable.

Japanese Fencers.

The luggage was placed on a tender; we took another boat, bade farewell to our steamer, and in a few minutes were standing on the soil of the Chrysanthemum Empire. Our luggage was then examined by the customs authorities in a quiet and efficient manner, quite different from the style in vogue at New York. I jumped into a *jinrikisha*—

my first experience of this style of conveyance—drawn by a little Jap on a full run, and was borne in no time to the Grand Hotel, where I had assigned to me a pleasant room looking out on the water in full view of the Sacred Mountain Fusiyama.

The next thing to do was to secure the services of a courier and guide, and I engaged an active little man named Ohashi to accompany me throughout my stay in the Mikado's dominions. Ohashi proposed that I should at once take a jinrikisha to visit the interesting sights of Yokohama, and I promptly acceded, the confinement and monotony of life on shipboard making this new experience highly welcome. We traveled through many interesting parts of the town; went to strange little theatres constructed of bamboo poles covered with matting, and saw performances of various kinds—wrestling, fencing, and at one place a gymnastic monkey troupe, whose simian artists were the most intelligent of their race I have ever seen. They were dressed like men, and wore masks to represent human faces. I felt almost like becoming a convert to the Darwinian theory. We saw also a woman in whose navel was inserted a whistle, which she blew as one would with the mouth; after which instrumentation she smoked a pipe by the same ingenious agency. Continuing on through the city, we visited several Buddhist and Shinto temples, and, as this was the first time that I had seen the heathen worshipping their idols, I was much interested.

By the time we returned it was quite dark, and the jinrikisha men stopped and lighted little paper lanterns, producing an effect that added forcibly to the strangeness of the scene. I got back a little before seven, and went in to dinner. The waiters at the Grand Hotel were of course Japanese. They were dressed in white linen jackets made without collars, dark-blue tights, and no shoes, but socks, called *tabi*, in which is fashioned a separate receptacle for the great toe.

Japanese servants are certainly rapid, noiseless, and effective. Thus well attended, and after an excellent dinner, with a bottle of Moet and Chandon, Imperial Brut, which I relished after my sea-voyage of two weeks, I took a jinrikisha, and, accompanied by my courier Ohashi, went for a ride around the town. The streets in the exclusively Japanese quarter were brilliantly illuminated with coloured lanterns, and were full of picturesqueness and activity. On our return we passed through the district assigned to houses of prostitution. These establishments are

Buddhist Priests, Japan

curiously arranged. The front is like a large cage, with wooden bars about two inches in thickness, and within these rooms are a row of unfortunate young girls from sixteen to nineteen years of age, dressed in showy and expensive gowns, squatting on their knees, with their hands clasped. They rarely speak, even to one another. These girls are bound by their parents to this horrible traffic for three years. When this time expires they go back to their homes, and usually marry and again become respectable members of society, according to Japanese conventions.

Monday morning, after an early breakfast, I visited several Japanese shops, and made purchases until I felt as if bankruptcy were staring me in the face. The temptation to buy overcomes the Occidental in Japan, where the bronze, lacquer-work, and embroideries are such marvels of

Fruit-selling in Yokohama

oddity, delicacy, and beauty, handicraft and art, as to be all but irresistible in their pull at the purse-strings.

After luncheon, or *tiffin*, as we must say here—and an excellent tiffin indeed—I rested for two hours, and then with the courier resumed the employment of the jinrikisha, and visited the Bluff, where are the houses of the Europeans. Many of these are beautiful and attractive. We now pushed on into the country, through many rice fields, where the natives were cutting and thrashing the rice, and returned after a tour of about ten miles. The jinrikisha men seemed as fresh as when they set out. Dinner followed; then a fresh ride about town, then bed and obliviousness.

Tattooing in Japan is a fine art. To the native it is now forbidden by law, but many foreigners, especially titled Englishmen, have specimens of dragons, serpents, and other strange designs worked on their arms and bodies by F. M. Harichiyo, who stands at the head of his profession in Yokohama. His charges are very high, some persons having paid as much as two thousand dollars for his handiwork. The Duke of Clarence, the Duke of York, Lord de Clifford, the Duke of Marlborough, and many officers of the Guards, have bestowed upon him their recommendations, which are recorded in a book he keeps for that purpose.

Tuesday morning I left Yokohama, with my guide, on the 9.20 train for Tokio. The country through which we passed was fertile, and devoted to the cultivation of rice, various kinds of fruit, and vegetables. The Japanese, like the Chinese, live almost entirely on rice, fish, eggs, chickens, and fruit. But few cattle, sheep, and horses are raised. Ploughs do not seem to be used at all, and carts rarely except in the "treaty ports." The native houses are uncomfortable in winter; the sides are made of soft paper, which is covered in bad weather by sliding panels of boards.

We arrived at the capital in about forty minutes from Yokohama, went at once to the Imperial Hotel, a large and excellent hostelry, deposited my luggage, and then continued on to the American legation for the purpose of getting my passport to visit the interior. The *chargé d'affaires*, Mr. Edwin Dun, most politely gave me much useful information for my guidance.

On my way back to the hotel I stopped at a Shinto temple, where, it being a *fête* day, a great crowd was present witnessing the ceremonies. Before saying their prayers in front of this shrine, the worshippers wash in a basin provided for that purpose, not their feet, as the Mohammedans do, but their hands, wiping them on small red and blue towels. They then proceed to the shrine, throw some small pieces of money into a box, pull a rope that rings a bell, drop on their knees and say their prayers. Many persons also bring offerings of fruit, rice, and the like. The priests remain near the altar, which is lighted with small candles, and their dress and mitres reminded me of their Roman Catholic brethren.

We soon left the temple and continued on our way back, passing the Imperial University, the Houses of Parliament, and the Club. I must acknowledge in this place the kindness of Mr. Peyton Jaudon, a New-Yorker, who has lived here for twenty-three years. Immediately after my arrival he showed me much politeness, and inscribed my name as a visitor at the Club, which is an excellent institution.

Shinto priest.

In Tokio I saw soldiers. Some in dress, manner, and traits are an exact copy of the German soldiers, while others resemble the French both in their training and their uniform. The cause of this difference is, that the instructors are French officers for some and Prussian for others. The troops are young, and, for Japanese, strong and large.

At 2 P. M. I set out for the garden party given by the Emperor at the Detached Palace. He arrived at about three, in a carriage thoroughly English in appearance, with servants dressed in English liveries, and an aid in magnificent uniform. The Emperor, attired in military uniform, was accompanied by all the important functionaries of the Government, and escorted by a detachment of lancers. The assemblage was brilliant, but was cut short by a heavy shower of rain.

I returned from the garden party through the grounds surrounding the Imperial Palace (which was burned April 5, 1872). The castle and garden are completely encircled by a very broad and deep moat, and the public are not admitted. A high stone wall is raised also to prevent access; and on the top of this wall, in certain places, are reared picturesque Japanese buildings. The whole effect is handsome and attractive. We also passed the superb residences of some of the wealthy nobility—all the structures being modern, and resembling splendid French châteaux. I was astounded at their size and grandeur; any one of them would be considered a palace in Newport. The Ginza, the principal street of Tokio, has a line of omnibuses and a tramway.

We stopped for an hour at the principal theatre and saw the play. A famous actor, the Henry Irving of his country, was performing. The theatre is large and comfortable, and resembles a European one, except that there are no seats. The audience all sit cross-legged on the floor. The performance begins at 11 A.M. and continues until 9 P.M. Between the acts meals are served in lacquered boxes, on trays, and tea is handed round. The meal of which my guide partook was rice and raw fish chopped fine and made into croquettes, and a species of glutinous seaweed rolled into balls and cooked. He ate it all with apparent relish. The scenery and the different curtains used—for there were several—were remarkably fine. The whole stage revolved, and by this means the scenery could be brought forward into use as wanted. After the theatre I went back to dinner. It rained, and I was glad of the occasion it gave me to seek an early bed.

The terrific earthquake of 1891 visited Japan on October 28th, ten days before my arrival there. This convulsion was the most disastrous in the history of the country since it has been opened to Europeans. The district affected was in the mountains, and the exact number of the killed and injured, and of the houses destroyed, will probably never be accurately known. In nearly all the towns the *débris* took fire and was completely consumed, which rendered it impossible for the people to rebuild their houses out of the same material. The official returns place the casualties at ten thousand people killed and injured, and about forty-seven thousand houses destroyed. In describing the part of the country where the earthquake happened I will give the result of my own observations after transcribing the following from the Japan Gazette:

"An earthquake occurred in Japan on the morning of October 28th, at about half past six, which proved the most disastrous seismic disturbance that has visited these islands for the last thirty-seven years. For some reason not quite obvious, seeing that violent earthquakes have by no means occurred at regular intervals, the Japanese expected some such calamity to befall the country on or about his Majesty the Emperor's birthday, November 3d; and it is a curious coincidence that the earthquake only anticipated the date assigned in these dismal apprehensions by seven days. The shock, as experienced in Yokohama and Tokio, was sufficiently sharp to be alarming in some degree, but although it lasted quite three minutes, little damage was done; the chimney of the Electric Light Company's works, a very top-heavy structure, and a not over-stalwart *godown* in China Town, being the sum total of damage in Yokohama, unless we may mention such trifles as the gold-fish in a garden pond being tossed on to the surrounding bank, and a few teacups being dislodged from shelves. In Tokio but little damage was done, though nineteen shocks in all were felt. The full force of the earthquake was experienced in Aichi and Gifu Kens, in Mino Province, about two hundred and twenty-five miles, in rough calculation, from the capital, situated on the Tokaido, along the south coast. The Jiji Shimpo publishes a correspondence from Gifu, dated Friday, October 30th, which is to the following effect:

"About a quarter to seven, on the morning of the 28th, a rumbling noise was heard, which was almost simultaneously followed by a violent shock, making the earth open in several places, and causing houses to fall in all directions; groans and shrieks from the terrified, the dying, and the wounded, filling the air. The direction of the motion appeared to be

Japanese wrestlers

from north-northeast to south-southeast. The violence of the shaking was really alarming, and almost every one felt as sick as if on board a vessel. The houses were completely brought down, their roofs lying on the ground, on both sides of the streets, the people passing to and fro over them in many cases, and finding great difficulty in making a way through the débris."

Wednesday morning was like a May day, warm and pleasant, and Ohashi and I, soon after breakfast, took jinrikishas and went directly to the Shiba temples. In my wildest dreams I had never thought that anything in Japan could be so beautiful as these temples and the park that surrounds them. Here are the tombs of the Shoguns. The lacquer-work, the carvings, the altars, are marvels of art. The park is beautifully kept, and the roads, like those in Tokio, are excellent. It is full of large trees of various kinds, but principally a variety of pine, which, instead of growing up vertically and mastlike as it does with us, spreads out like an English oak.

From Shiba Park we went across the street to a curious bazaar, and then on to the Maple-wood Club. This is a large building, of many rooms, made entirely of maple wood, as its name indicates, in Japanese style, where select parties have their entertainments. The surrounding grounds are attractive and contain many handsome cherry, maple, and camphor trees. The display of cherry blossoms here in the spring is said to be superb. We partook of tea and some curious pink cakes made of uncooked rice, flour, and sugar, dried in the oven but not baked.

Here, as at the Shiba temples, we were obliged to take off our shoes and leave them outside, following the example of the natives, and walking in our stocking-feet. We left the Maple Club reluctantly, and directed our way to the place where the forty-seven Rônins lie buried together in a certain division of a cemetery. Incense is burned here constantly, and on certain feast-days many persons leave their visiting-cards on Oishi Kuranosuke's grave. A Rônin was a man of gentle blood, who had become separated from the prince to whom he owed allegiance. Attachment to such a master was the leading passion of a retainer's life, and appreciation of such devotion was the highest sentiment of national honour. A Rônin was privileged to bear arms, and when Fate had cast him adrift he became a sort of knight-errant. Men would sometimes become Rônins in order to exempt their lords from the penalty attached to some deed of blood.

At the beginning of the eighteenth century an ambassador was sent from the Mikado to the lord of the Castle of Ako, whose title was " Barbarian-repressing-Commander-in-Chief." Takumi no Kami and another noble, Kaimei Sama, were appointed to entertain him, and a high officer named Kotsuke no Suke was named to teach them the necessary ceremonies to be observed. The two noblemen were compelled to go to the castle every day and be instructed. As the lessons progressed, Suke received, as was customary, a present from each nobleman in recognition of his services. He was a greedy soul, and, thinking the rewards contemptible, he turned the instruction into ridicule, and Kaimei Sama, who was the more violent of the two, determined to kill Suke. When the ceremonies were ended and Sama had returned to his palace, he summoned his followers and in secret conference told of the insults that had been put upon him and his companion. He added: " I thought to kill Suke upon the spot, but reflected that not only should I lose my life, but my family and vassals would be ruined. Still, I have now resolved that, come what will, he must die by my hand." Among the retainers was a discreet man, who saw that remonstrance was useless, so he said: " Your words are law; your servants will prepare themselves. To-morrow, if Suke comes to the court, treat him according to your wishes." Sama longed for dawn, that he might execute his purpose, but the counsellor went home heavy-hearted. After reflection on the matter, he decided to save his master and the household. He collected all the money he could and went to Suke's palace, and addressed his retainers in these words: " My master, who is now occupied in the entertainment of the imperial envoy, owes much thanks to Lord Kotsuke no Suke. He sends but a shabby present, but hopes his lordship will condescend to accept it." Kotsuke sent with delighted eagerness for the counsellor to come to his inner chamber, and after thanking him, promised on the morrow to be more careful than ever in his instruction on every point of etiquette. When Kaimei arrived he found the manner of Suke so changed that his heart gradually softened, and he renounced his idea of killing him. When Takumi no Kami followed, Suke ridiculed him, but he took no apparent notice of the insults. Finally, Suke said haughtily, " My sock-ribbon has

Grand Hotel, Yokohama.

come untied; be so good as to tie it, my Lord of Takumi." Takumi was in an inward frenzy, but believed that, as he was on duty, he must obey. As he did so Suke said: " Why, how clumsy you are! Any one can see that you are a boor, and know nothing of the fashions in Yeddo." As he spoke he moved away. " Stop a moment, my lord," said Kami. " Well, for what?" said Suke. Kami drew a dirk from his belt and aimed a blow at him. Suke, saved by his court cap, retreated. Kami chased him, and missing his aim, struck his dirk into a pillar just as a court officer came upon the scene, and Suke escaped. A council decided that Takumi no Kami, for thus disturbing the peace, must perform *hara-kiri*, that his castle must be confiscated, and his retainers become Rónins. Among them was one called Oishi Kuranosuke, who with forty-six others formed a sacred compact to kill Kotsuke no Suke. They laid many plans, but Kotsuke was so well guarded that there was no hope except in strategy. To effect this they separated, and, disguised as carpenters or merchants, or other tradesmen, pursued their various callings. Kuranosuke, the leader, gave himself up to drunkenness and evil ways, until the passers-by sneered at him, and his wife separated from him amid bitter reproaches. One day a Satsuma man, seeing him in the gutter, called him a fool and a craven, who had not the heart to avenge his lord, and was unworthy of a soldier's name. Then he spat on him and trod on his face, without moving the insensate Kuranosuke. Kotsuke no Suke's spies carried this news to their lord, and he felt that certainly all danger was over. Meantime the carpenters and other workmen had, in the way of their callings, found entrance into Suke's palace and become familiar with its arrangement and customs. At last Kuranosuke believed that the time had arrived. In the depth of winter he fled secretly from Yeddo, rallied his followers, and the attack was planned. When all was ready, Oishi Kuranosuke made two speeches to the Rónins, saying: "To-night we shall attack our enemy in his palace; his retainers will certainly resist us, and we shall be obliged to kill them; but to slay old men and women and children is a pitiful thing; therefore I pray you to take great heed lest you kill a single helpless person." By a messenger he sent the following to the neighbouring houses:

"We, the Rónins, who were formerly in the service of Asano Takumi no Kami, are this night about to break into the palace of Kotsuke no Suke to avenge our lord. As we are neither night robbers nor ruffians, no hurt will be done to the neighbouring homes."

The neighbours had no love for Kotsuke no Suke, and nothing in such an enterprise was to be feared from them. The Rônins forced an entrance to the palace, and fought step by step until every man in Suke's household was slain. Occasionally Takumi's men wavered, but the daring leader was everywhere, cheering them on and keeping the one end in view. From one hiding-place to another they hunted the helpless chieftain. At last Kuranosuke dragged him forth, and thus addressed him:

"My lord, we are the retainers of Asano Takumi no Kami. Last year your lordship and our master quarrelled in the palace, and our master was sentenced to *hara-kiri*, and his family were ruined. We have come to-night to avenge him, as is the duty of faithful and loyal men. I pray your lordship to acknowledge the justice of our purpose. And now, my lord, we beseech you to perform *hara-kiri*. I myself shall have the honour to act as your second; and when, with all humility, I shall have received your lordship's head, it is my intention to lay it as an offering upon the grave of Asano Takumi no Kami." But the cowering nobleman had not will enough left to die that death deemed worthy of his rank, and so Kuranosuke cut off his head and bore it away in triumph. Before leaving, the Rônins extinguished the lights and fires, lest an accident should endanger the neighbourhood. Their way to the town was a triumphal march, such was the admiration felt for them as soon as the cause for the strange procession was explained. Then they called for the priests to burn incense, and begged that, when they had committed *hara-kiri*, the money which was handed to the priests should be used in masses. This done, they patiently waited the inevitable sentence from the supreme authority. This was the order that they expected, and the faithful retainers killed themselves with quiet dignity. They numbered forty-seven, but forty-eight upright stones are seen by the traveller. The Satsuma man, in repentant sorrow, committed *hara-kiri*, and was buried with the Rônins.

Returning home, I had tiffin, and then went to the chrysanthemum show. This was indeed a curious sight. There was a narrow street, and abutting on it were numerous gardens, in which were grottoes and theatrical stages, some of which revolved as they do in the Japanese theatres. On these were arranged, in a representation of historical or

Chrysanthemum images, Kioto.

fabulous scenes, lay figures, whose clothing was composed of growing chrysanthemums. For instance, in one place there was a daimio being dragged off a horse by the devil — all the figures being of life-size, and fashioned in growing flowers. I also saw a choice collection of the miniature trees that are peculiar to Japan. I take the description from an excellent authority :

Pagoda at Ueno.

"Japan is the home of the best varieties of chrysanthemums, as it is of the dwarf orange tree, and of oaks a century old in six-inch pots. The highest distinction the Mikado can confer upon any of his subjects is the decoration of the chrysanthemum. The chrysanthemum is also the royal seal, and for centuries has been esteemed and loved by the people, nobles, and commons. When we think of the slow growth of varieties in garden flowers, how long the single rose must have been cultivated, and variations noted and fostered, before we had the immense full double sorts now known, we must believe that it is centuries since the careful Chinese and Japanese gardeners began to improve the chrysanthemum from the little single flower which is supposed to be the original of all the varieties now in cultivation.

"The Japanese guard the choicest flowers with jealous care, and it is possible that varieties are carefully cultivated in some part of the empire that are superior to those known to Occidentals. It is even believed by travellers that in some part of either China or Japan exists that fabulous flower, the blue chrysanthemum. Chrysanthemums of blue are figured on old porcelain and mentioned in written works."

Miss Scidmore, in her book, "Jinrikisha Days in Japan," says that in the house of the head man of the village of Kawana, the possessor of a wonderful collection of chrysanthemums, she was given a salad made from the petals of yellow chrysanthemums. It is also said that the Japanese put the petals of the flower into the *sake* cup to prolong life and keep free from misfortunes. It is possible that the resinous quality of the flower has some hidden virtue not generally known.

Leaving the chrysanthemum show, we proceeded to Ueno Park, a lovely spot, and visited the Museum, where I saw the ancient bullock-cart and palanquins that were formerly used by the Mikados. These vehicles are made of richly ornamented ebony, and hung with curtains designed to prevent any one from seeing the august occupants, who were considered sacred and worshipped as gods. Even at present the

Mikado is regarded with devout veneration by the adherents of Shintoism, he being the head of their religion, in much the same relation as that of the Czar to the Russian Church.

There were many other curiosities to be seen, of various kinds; among them the relics of the Christians who here underwent martyrdom in the seventeenth century. Passing from these to the zoölogical de-

Cherry Blossoms at Ueno Park.

partment, we pursued our way to Asakusa to see its temples and the park, comprising, in our trip, in catholic impartiality, a number of shows of jugglery, acrobats, and performing dogs.

Crossing on our way the Great River, we returned to the hotel, and after dinner resumed jinrikishas, tandem this time, and set out for a tour around the city, passing through Yoshiwara, where there are innumerable bagnios inhabited by several thousand women. Some of their establishments are like enormous hotels, four stories high, and with a frontage of a hundred feet on the street.

Thursday morning, at 8.50, we took up our course for Nikko. The country on each side seemed to be rich and well tilled, producing tea, mulberry trees, and, of course, a deal of rice. Around fields dotted with the invariably thatched cottages are fences of bamboo, or hedges; and in all directions spread the splendid cryptomeria trees. We arrived at our destination in the afternoon at two o'clock.

A Japanese Game.

Japanese Idols.

CHAPTER III.

IN JAPAN.

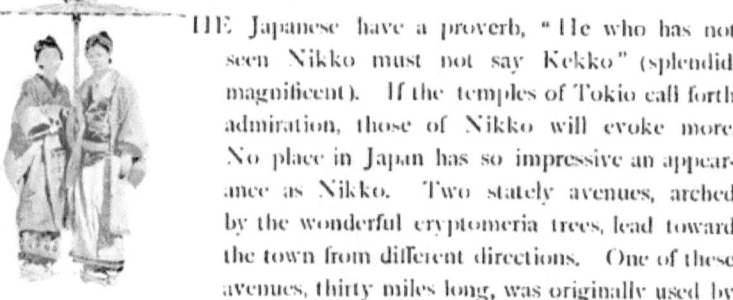

THE Japanese have a proverb, "He who has not seen Nikko must not say Kekko" (splendid, magnificent). If the temples of Tokio call forth admiration, those of Nikko will evoke more. No place in Japan has so impressive an appearance as Nikko. Two stately avenues, arched by the wonderful cryptomeria trees, lead toward the town from different directions. One of these avenues, thirty miles long, was originally used by the Mikado's envoy on his way from Kioto to pay homage at the shrine. Here are the tombs of two mighty rulers, Ieyasu and Iyemitsu. Ieyasu, the first Shogun of the Tokugawa family, was by a strange coincidence a contemporary of Oliver Cromwell, and, like him, he changed an empire and crystallized a government. Ieyasu's government was more enduring than the great Protector's; it lasted two hundred and fifty years, Ieyasu being ably succeeded by his grandson, whose tomb is also in this place. We stand in silent wonder before the beautiful lacquerwork and lifelike carvings of birds and foliage cut from wood.

On Friday morning I went early to the temples, which are near the Nikko Hotel, and carefully examined them all. The grounds in which they are situated are almost the finest I have ever seen, and around these on all sides grow the noble cryptomeria trees. The temples are far more elaborate than those which I so much admired in Shiba Park. The carvings are marvellous, and the different kinds of lacquer astonishingly beautiful. To reproduce them, if such a thing were possible, would cost many millions of dollars.

The temple used as the stable of the sacred white pony Jimme was curious as well as interesting. At one time, so I was told, more than

Stable of the sacred white pony.

three thousand priests were employed here, Buddhist and Shinto. Now there are but fifty. The interest in religious matters seems to be dying out to a great extent, and among the educated class are many agnostics and atheists. The argument of the Japanese in favour of their present religion is difficult to answer. They acknowledge the good points of Christianity, but claim that all religions are good in theory, and that to estimate them rightly it is necessary to investigate their effect on the people. They say, and with undoubted truth, that in Christian countries there is much more vice, drunkenness, discontent, and misery than in Japan; therefore, to judge from the results, it is inexpedient to change. The Japanese are friendly to the Christian religion; they do not attempt to persecute converts to Christianity or to interfere with them, and indeed are entirely free from bigotry and intolerance. In this respect their example to the missionaries should be good. They are an amiable, polite, and contented people; and are certainly the cleanliest of all nationalities. A curious old Buddhist proverb says: "A woman's exterior is that of a saint, but her heart is that of a demon." This, I am sure, is untrue as regards the modern women of Japan. They are apparently all that can be desired.

I believe that under the law women have more rights at present in Japan than in any European country. In former times they were practically the property of their husbands. They have one hardship to contend with, though, if no other. At night, instead of a pillow, a little wooden box serves as a prop for their necks and heads, to prevent the disarrangement of their hair, which is dressed very elaborately and but once a week.

Coming out, after tiffin, on the veranda of the hotel, on this same day, we found a number of dealers in curios and furs, with their goods displayed, in hopes of effecting sales to the guests. This is the principal fur-producing part of Japan, and fine, well-tanned beaver, otter, marten, antelope, and monkey skins can be bought for ridiculously low prices. For instance, a dollar and a quarter (about equal to an American dollar) will buy a handsome beaver skin, and a fine otter skin can be had for four dollars.

We took jinrikishas and went to Kamman-go-fuchi, on the river Daiyagawa, which is here a boiling mountain stream. The place is lovely in its scenery, surrounded in all directions by the Nikkozan Mountains. Rising by the riverside, straight out of a deep pool, is a rock bearing a Sanscrit inscription. Tradition declares that Kobo-

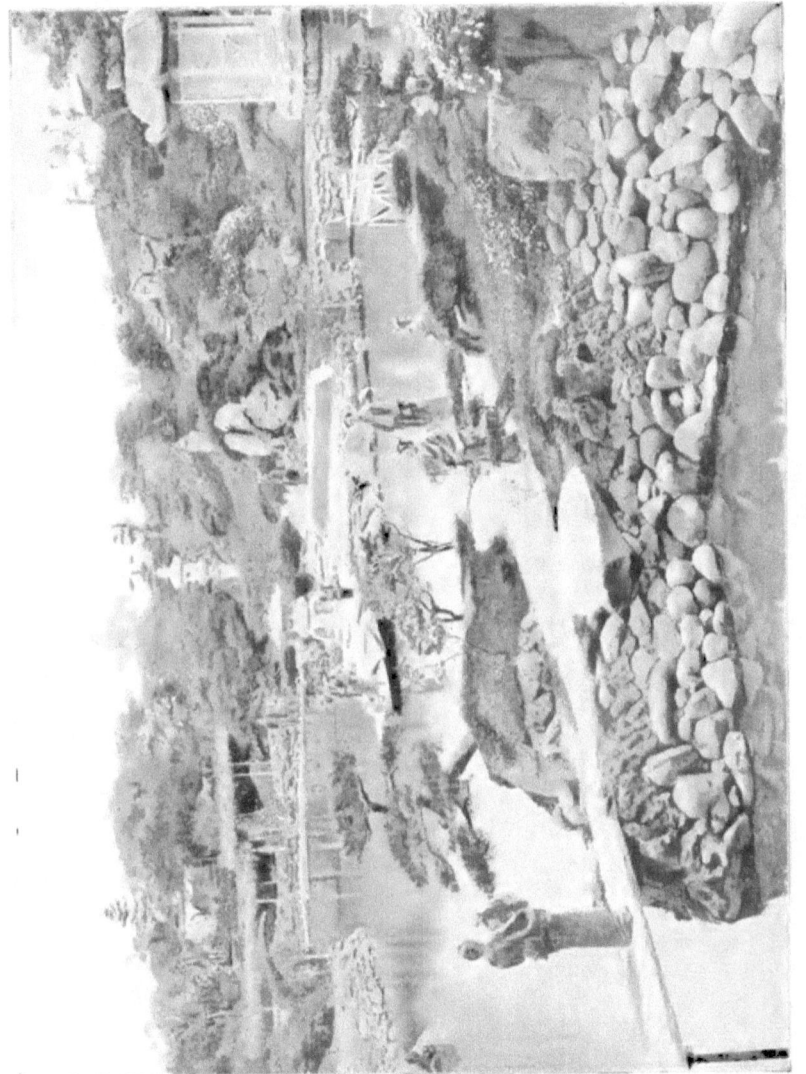

Garden at Nikko.

Daishi once threw his pen across the river, and by this pen the inscription was miraculously graven on the rock. On the bank of the river also stands a long row of images of Amida. It is impossible, so it is said, to count these images correctly.

We visited Dainichi-do, where are a beautiful garden, miniature lake, and tea-house. Taking another way back, we passed two curious

The images of Amida.

little mills for grinding rice and barley. The flume of each was about two feet wide, and the wheel was something smaller than a good-sized cart wheel.

At Yumoto are ten hot springs, some in the open air and others in bath-houses. They are open to all, and men and women go in together, entirely naked, without the least thought of impropriety. The Japanese are inveterate splashers. They all take a hot bath every morning. The water is almost at the boiling-point, but they seem to be able to stand it. Each house has a wooden box in the floor, which answers for the bath-tub, and the family get in, each member in succession, without changing the water.

The manager of the Nikko Hotel informed me that he had spent five years in the United States—two at Rutgers College, and three in San

Japanese girls.

Francisco in the employ of the Chicago and Northwestern Railway. From him I received considerable information in regard to the railway system of Japan. The railways are mainly owned by the Government,

although some branch lines are owned by companies. They are narrow-gauge, the stations being after the French and German fashion. The rate of speed is only about twenty miles an hour, but everything appertaining to them is managed remarkably well.

Friday was a warm and lovely November day. It was just one month since I had left New York, now eight thousand miles distant. At 8.30 we set out with tandem jinrikishas for Lake Chuzenji. Our way lay along the side of a small, swift stream, at the bottom of a deep ravine, with mountains towering overhead, and soon we were climbing the mountain side. The path was steep, but in good condition. Annually during August it is trodden by about twenty thousand pilgrims on their way to shrines and sacred images on the top of Nantai-zan, a steep mountain near the lake. We stopped at several tea-houses to rest the men, and partook of tea and queer-looking lollypops. At one of them I saw several bird-cages, each with a solitary occupant. On the outside of its cage was a small stick serving for a perch, covered with an adhesive gum. The bird in the cage attracted his fellows of the trees to alight upon the perch, where their feet would stick so tightly that the flutterers could be caught with ease. There are many women in these mountains who continue the old practice of blackening their teeth immediately after marriage. But this fashion, which transforms a good-looking woman into a hag, is rapidly waning. Near Lake Chuzenji are copper mines, and we met many horses loaded with the ingots. These horses are without metal on their feet, which are shod only with straw. Resuming our course, we went down a steep declivity into a superb gorge, to look at the beautiful Kegon-no-taki Falls, in which there is one drop of three hundred and fifty feet. We arrived soon afterward at Lake Chuzenji. There we went for tiffin to a tea-house, where I was served with a piece of excellent salmon, nicely fried, good bread and butter, some fruit, and a cup of saké, the only alcoholic liquor made or used by the natives. Unlike wine, brandy, and whisky, it is considered better when quite new. It is a brew of rice, and the Japanese serve it hot at the beginning of dinner. The best quality is exceedingly pleasant to the taste. It resembles a very light dry sherry or manzanilla. That which I had at Chuzenji I found especially good. I have wondered if the diet of the

Idol at Nikko.

Japanese has not had an influence on their dispositions. They live almost entirely on vegetables, with a few fish or eggs occasionally; meat they virtually never touch. They are mild-mannered, polite, orderly, and clean, and they have a great regard for the rights of others. In habits, the people most directly their opposite are the English, who eat enormous quantities of meat and drink largely of spirits, and who are, as every one knows, great bullies, both individually and as a nation. It is fortunate for the Japanese that they have reached a point in civilization where it is not likely that England, France, or Russia can seize their country on some flimsy pretext, as might have been done years ago.

My table was spread on the pretty little veranda of the paper-sided tea-house, which is directly on the lake. The lake is small, but very picturesque, surrounded with sharp-peaked hills densely covered to the water's edge with foliage, of which the autumn tints vied with anything on Lake George or the Hudson River. My day of excursion to Chuzenji will always dwell in my memory as a most charming one. We returned to the hotel in about half the time that we had occupied in going, and I had an opportunity to revisit the wonderful temples before four o'clock, the hour at which the gates are closed.

On Sunday, at 7.20, a frosty but fine morning, we left Nikko and returned to Tokio, arriving at the Imperial Hotel at about 1 P.M.

Japanese lady in chair.

At tiffin the son of the late deposed Tycoon was present, dressed like a European gentleman. His private fortune is large, but he is shorn of all political power. It must seem strange to the older

Japanese, who remember the condition of affairs before any innovations arose in their country, to see the Mikado, and him who should have been the Tycoon—princely personages, all of whose ancestors were once esteemed as sacred—acting and dressing like Europeans. Matters have changed indeed in Japan. It is as if the Pope should put on a tweed suit and go to the Derby, or dance the cotillion at a ball. In Tokio I saw, among other curious things, gold-fish with fluted tails and the remarkable Tosa chickens, in the museum. One of these chickens had tail-feathers eighteen feet long.

I had the pleasure of meeting a Union Club man, Mr. W. Stanard Wood, who was making a tour of the world with his bride.

Having rested awhile at the hotel, I went again to Asakusa. Here are some remarkable temples, but after Nikko they did not impress me as when I saw them first. In one that we entered eight Buddhist priests were holding a service for the repose of the souls of those killed in the recent earthquake. I could not but notice a close resemblance to the accessories of Christian church service—in the chancel, altar, incense, and lighted candles, in the golden flowers in vases, in the tolling of the bell for all to bow their heads, in the bending of the knees as the worshippers passed the altar, in the sing-song voices of the priests, and, I may add, in the congregation itself, almost entirely composed of old women on their knees telling their beads.

When I discovered the object of the service I sent my guide with a contribution of five yen ($3.67), which delighted both priests and worshippers. They sent me a receipt, in Japanese, and the man who occupied the position equivalent to that of sexton brought us two chairs and some tea-cakes and candied fruit for our refreshment; and when we left several of the congregation came down the steps and made us profound obeisances.

We then went into the Asakusa Kōenchi or public park that surrounds the temple. Here are to be found all sorts of tea-houses, restaurants, shops for the sale of cheap toys and confectionery, jugglers, and other shows too many to name. The spectacle reminded me somewhat

Koro at Nikko.

of the Prater in Vienna on a Sunday afternoon. We did not tarry long; the crowd was great, and I had already been through the place pretty thoroughly. We returned through the Ginza, the Oxford Street or Broadway of Tokio.

On Monday morning I left Tokio at 9.30, reaching Yokohama in less than an hour, and again put up at the Grand Hotel. On the train thither a brakeman rushed in and closed all the blinds on one side of the car. On inquiry I was informed that the Empress Dowager was passing in another train.

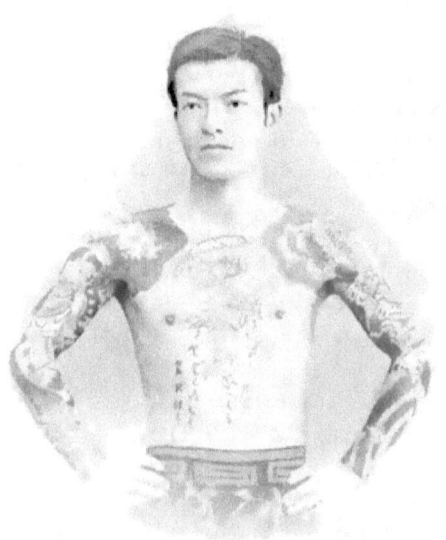

Immediately on our alighting at the hotel, Ohashi, the guide, was informed that his wife that morning had given birth to a child. He was quite upset at the tidings of this blessing. The little visitant was not indeed unexpected, but as Ohashi already had four infants to support, the latest comer was not as welcome as his first-born had been. However, on learning that it was a boy Ohashi's spirits revived somewhat; and in view of the circumstances I gave him two days to set matters right in his household.

A strange phenomenon was called to my attention; it seems that the seeds in the persimmon are upside down this year. The old people say this was so thirty-seven years ago, the time of the great earthquake. It seems certainly convenient that a terrible upheaval of nature should be foretold in this unmistakable way.

After tiffin I went to the studio of F. M. Harichiyo and selected a design of a dragon to be tattooed on my arm. He began operations at 2 P. M. and continued working rapidly until 1 A. M., with an intermission of only one hour for dinner—ten hours of steady work from high daylight until past midnight. It was very painful, as each puncture of the skin brought blood; but the result was most satisfactory. Tuesday I spent in resting quietly, and recuperating from the effects of the tattooing.

On Wednesday morning I bade farewell to Yokohama and took the train to Fuji-sawa, going thence by jinrikisha to the temple of Hachiman, and also to the Daibutzu or Great Buddha. This remarkable statue stands in grounds beautifully laid out. Its height is nearly fifty feet, the thumb being three feet in circumference. The eyes are of gold, and the rest of the image is constructed of bronze plate about an inch thick. A door leads into the interior of the statue, which contains a shrine. Formerly a temple stood adjacent to the image. This temple was destroyed by a tidal wave in 1369. It was rebuilt, and was again destroyed by the same agency in 1494, and has not been reconstructed.

We went to the Temple of Kwannon, which is on an eminence overlooking the sea. Here is a huge image thirty feet high, carved from one camphor-wood tree. It is inside the temple, and in darkness until the attendant priest lights a few candles, and with a small rope attached to the roof hoists up the visitor that he may see the lacquering of the figure.

We went thence to the Kaihai-in Hotel at Kamakura, which is directly on the seashore, and in summer is a popular bathing resort. We had tiffin, and then wended our way along the edge of the sea to Enoshima, a lovely, picturesque island, which when the tide is out is connected with the mainland in much the same manner as is Mount-Saint-Michel, in France; but here, instead of a solid causeway, like that at Mount-Saint-Michel, there is a long plank walk, supported on bamboo poles, which is recurrently washed away. Enoshima is accessible in all directions by means of narrow paths, and the walk and steps on the way to the celebrated cavern are cut out of solid rock.

This cave is nearly four hundred feet in depth, and the sea flows into it. At the extreme end is a Shinto temple, and the priest lighted us through the dark passage. Returning to the station, we went by train to Kozu, and from that point to Yumoto, a journey of about an hour and a half by tram car. On alighting, I took jinrikishas for Miyanoshita. It was quite dark when we arrived, and the first view of the Fuji-ya Hotel was startling, as its sides are all of glass, and they were ablaze with electric lights. The visitor to Japan is still imperfectly prepared to encounter all its modern conveniences.

In the morning I had a splendid bath in water from the natural hot springs. Every adjunct of the bath room was neat and satisfactory, and the bath, though very hot, was very enjoyable.

One thing is peculiarly pleasant to the traveller in Japan: there are none of those exasperating extra charges for lights, candles, attendants, linen, fires, etc., which in a European trip goad the victim to frenzy, the

Cave at Enoshima.

ostensible "main" charges being only one tentacle on the radiates of an octopus.

I left the hotel at 8.30, with Ohashi, and in chairs, on the shoulders of two coolies, we proceeded up the mountain. In some places the ascent was very difficult; but the men, although small and without the appearance of strength, carried us up seemingly with perfect ease. At exactly

Famous mineral baths, Miyanshita.

11.45, in cool, bright, and clear sunshine, we arrived at the top of Otometoge, or Virgin's Pass, where the view of the sacred mountain Fusiyama was perfect. It showed itself in its full grandeur, and opposite the mighty cone the silver waters of Lake Hakone, in the beautiful valley, and the steam from the boiling springs of Ojigoku were distinctly discernible.

We spent more than an hour here, and took tiffin, which we had brought with us, adding to it some tea, obtained from the little

The cave at Enoshima.

nest-built house that has been placed at this spot for the use of travellers.

At one tea-house I was surprised—so far was it up the mountain side, and away from any settlement—to see eight boys and girls about eight years old each with a small baby strapped to the back, in the Japanese fashion. The parents were busy in the mountain side, and had brought their children up with them. Among the poor the house-mother continually fastens one child on the shoulders of its little brother or sister, who carries the baby thus all day, apparently with uncomplaining philosophy. About four o'clock we got back to Miyanoshita, and walked through the village, in which are many shops. We looked into one of the Japanese bath-houses. Here were sixteen people, all naked, sitting in the hot water—men, women, and some small children—while more people—an old woman, a little girl, and two boys—were just about crowding themselves into the bath-box in the floor. The quaint, slant-eyed, amiable bathers were undisturbed by the presence of a spectator at the open door. In the evening, before going to bed, I received a shampooing in my room, at the hands of a blind old woman with a close-shaven head. It seemed strange at first, but so, at first, does everything.

On Friday morning, November 20th, we retraced our course, going in jinrikishas to Yumoto, there taking the tram-car to Kozu and its railway station, and thence the cars for Shizuoka, where we went to the Daito-Kwan Hotel. No English was spoken in this house. The country along the route is fine, rich land, and it is irrigated, in common with a great part of Japan, for the cultivation of rice. Tea and rice are produced here too. To us in the United States, where irrigation is in its beginning, an investigation of the Japanese system by competent persons would, I should think, be of great value.

We passed near the base of Fusiyama, which looked imposing. The mountain's height is said to be fourteen thousand feet; in summer it is comparatively easy of ascent, but in November the snow is too deep.

The interior of the hotel at Shizuoka was arranged as is usual in Japanese houses, the whole floor being divided into innumerable rooms by means of panels, which can be removed to leave larger compartments, or to throw the whole floor into one room. These panels have no locks or fastenings of any kind, so that it is possible to walk into an adjoining room without difficulty. This, however, it seems, is never done, being forbidden by some unwritten law.

We set out from Shizuoka by train at 6 A.M. for Nagoya. The country between these towns is perfectly flat, with mountains on one

Nagoya

side and the sea on the other. It was entirely devoted to farming, but, as is the case everywhere in Japan, one sees few domestic animals, the natives making no use of sheep, pigs, or cattle for food. A few horses are visible in some localities, ploughing and carrying packs. Bullocks

A View of Fusiyama.

also are sometimes employed in the same way. The feeling still prevails that an animal may contain the soul of some ancestor or friend. But many black bullocks—controlled by wooden rings in the nose, which seem to hold them securely—are used in the vicinity of Kioto to draw queer-looking carts.

At 12.35 P. M. on Saturday, November 21st, we arrived at Nagoya. On all sides were evidences of the terrible earthquake that had taken place so recently—the ground cracked open, many houses entirely thrown to the ground, others partially wrecked, and many that were standing propped up with poles. We went to the Shinachū Hotel, a semi-European house, which was comparatively uninjured, but all the environment was a scene of devastation. Shocks still continued every day, and I felt one that afternoon. On October 28th, the day when the great damage was done, the earth rose and fell eighteen inches. Many people were killed, and the terror of the inhabitants beggars description.

In the afternoon I went out in a jinrikisha, saw the castle and the two beautiful golden dolphins on the top of a pagoda-like tower, and visited a temple and a manufactory of porcelain and cloisonné, where I was much interested in the curious processes employed. At eleven o'clock that night I was roused from sleep with a start. A smart shock of earthquake had awakened me. The disturbance soon ceased, without damage to the hotel, which was propped up outside with long poles.

On Sunday morning, November 22d, we left Nagoya with four jinrikishas; one for myself, one for my guide, and the others for my luggage, each of the four being drawn by two men. We took our course through the city, and then followed the old Tokaido road. Again our way lay amid ruins. The road was almost impassable in some places on account of earthquake cracks, some of them several feet wide. We brought our food with us, and stopped for tiffin at a tea-house that had been re-erected on its old site. So on we crossed Kisogawa River in a large flat-boat, taking the jinrikishas with us.

On the opposite shore a small village had been entirely destroyed. Nothing was left, for its *debris* had taken fire after the shock.

Japanese dancing girls.

CHAPTER IV.

FAREWELL TO JAPAN.

AT three o'clock we arrived at Gifu, the centre of the earthquake district. We left our luggage at the Tsŭno-Kuni-ya Hotel, and with the same men as before — for they did not seem in the least fatigued after their run of twenty-five miles — we made a tour of the city, in one part of which the house-owners were diligently rebuilding homes that had been consumed by fire. Great distress exists throughout this part of the country, for the people in many instances have lost everything except what they had on their persons. One of the customary sights of Gifu is the fishing with cormorants. We went to see these birds, but I found to my regret that they had all been sent up the Nagara, out of harm's way.

Returning to the hotel, I found it to be exclusively in the "Japanese style," and was obliged to take off my shoes and put on slippers before

Principal street in Ozaki after the great earthquake.

entering. A room in a little wooden pavilion in the garden was assigned to me. There were but two rooms, both on the ground, so that it was possible to vacate them speedily in case of a shock. The house was as clean as possible, with sliding paper panels, which in summer perhaps are comfortable, but are decidedly cool at night in November. We had brought cold chicken, beef, bread, beer, etc., and with the addition of boiled eggs and rice I had a good dinner. At about 8.30 P. M. all the Japanese turned in, and I followed suit. Bedding was laid on the floor, with two thick "comfortables" for covering. The ensuing hours were not wholly pleasant, however, for my Japanese neighbours kept up an incessant talking all night, and in addition to this there was one tremendous shock of earthquake, which demolished the few tottering houses that had remained standing, and several lesser throes occurred. There was but one bath-tub and one wash-bowl for the hotel, and the guests, except me, all got into this tub without changing the water. I contented myself with the use of the wash-bowl, having warm water which was clean.

On Monday, at 8.30 A. M., we resumed our journey, in jinrikishas. The scene of desolation and destruction through which we passed was even more terrible than on the previous day. In some places the road was almost impassable for the huge holes and cracks left by the earthquake. In front of the ruins were little notices telling the number of deaths in each house.* At one place we stopped to see a Japanese doctor treating the wounded, assisted by two Japanese nurses dressed in white, with caps on which were red Genevan crosses. We reached Ozaki at 11.15 A. M., in time to take the train that was about to start for Kioto. The railway station at Ozaki and the whole village were in ruins, but beyond that point the evidences of seismal convulsions came suddenly to an end. At Tarui, two or three miles from Ozaki, there

* "Our hopes that the distressed districts had escaped the shocks of earthquake experienced here during the past few days have not, we regret to say, been realized, for a telegram from Gifu states that strong shocks were felt on Sunday night, bringing down many of the partially demolished buildings. Poor Gifu!"— *Japan Gazette, November 24, 1891.*

was no sign whatever of the upheaval that had done such deadly work behind us. The train took us into an excellent agricultural country, especially on the border of Lake Biwa. Otsu, through which we passed, is famous for its giant pine tree, which I saw later, and is also notable as the place where an insane policeman attempted the life of the czarewitch on May 11, 1891.

We arrived at Kioto about 3.30 P. M., and went at once to the Kioto Hotel, a large one, well kept in European style, where I found a pleasant bed-room and parlour. At dinner, bamboo sprouts (and I found them excellent) were among the vegetables. It was a national *fête* day, and the streets through which I went in the evening were adorned with paper lanterns.

On Tuesday morning, November 2d, a bright and sunny day, we set out, as usual, at 8.30, in jinrikishas, with two men to each, for the Rapids of Katsuragōwa. After leaving Kioto we went along a mountain road amidst lovely scenery, passed through a long tunnel, and thence downward to Hōzu, where we began the descent of the rapids. There was ready for us a skiff about forty feet long, managed by four men, to whom we added our party of six, taking the jinrikishas with us. The bed of the river is rocky, and it was wonderful with what skill the boatmen guided us down the swift current. The descent required just two hours. The scenery is beautiful. On both sides, for about thirteen miles, extend steep hills, the habitat of many large monkeys. At 1.30 we reached Arashi-yama. Here we landed and went to a pleasant tea house, and I partook of the tiffin I had brought from Kioto.

The Japanese have an excellent and inexpensive way of banking up the sides of rivers by means of open-work baskets of split bamboo about one hundred feet long, which are filled with stones taken from the river. By laying one of these baskets on another the artisans construct a strong wall, at much less outlay than for an equal mass of stone and cement, especially a subaqueous one.

After dinner I visited a Japanese theatre, and saw some curious dancing. The dancers, wearing very rich and handsome dresses, kept time, in slow and graceful movements, to the music of flutes, guitars, and small drums, played by twelve Japanese girls.

Wednesday, November 25th, I devoted to the sights of Kioto. The various temples are large and beautiful, but the absence of lacquer on the outside makes them appear at disadvantage in comparison with those at Nikko and Tokio. I ascended the Yasaka

A guitar-player.

Pagoda, which is the highest in the country, and from its top I had a splendid view of the city. The great Buddha or Daibutsu here I also visited. It is a huge wooden image, but not so fine as the one at Kama-Kura. It was festival day at the Shinto temples, being the 25th of the month, and at one of these I stopped and witnessed the functions in which about twenty-five priests, dressed in white and light blue, with black mitres, received presents of fish, fruit, poultry, and vegetables from the people.

At Kurodani I was shown two pine trees whose branches are so trained out on bamboo poles that one of them looks like a fan and the other like an umbrella. The cemetery adjoining this temple is very beautiful and commands a splendid view. In visiting these superb and costly religious structures, which it has cost so much money for ages to erect and to maintain, I could not, in admiring their beauties, lose the sense of the enormous waste of expenditure. That this money might better have been used for the people's education and elevation than in honouring the gods of the heathen imagination, is an Occidental and modern idea. Japan, however, is becoming modernized.

The palace of the Mikado I viewed, of course. The buildings are enclosed with a high wall, and the surroundings, with the view of the mountains, are very beautiful. The interior of the palace is extremely plain, and entirely Japanese in arrangement. I visited also several manufactories of silk, porcelain, and embroidery.

On Thursday I continued my visits to the temples, going first to the Higashi Hongwanji, which is in process of building. It is a renewal, the former temple having been destroyed by fire in 1864. The present edifice — the only instance of modern temple building that I have witnessed — will be the largest and probably the handsomest in all Japan. Several million dollars have been expended already in the construction of this pile. Labour upon it was begun about twenty years ago, and much more may be required before it is finished. The funds have been raised by voluntary subscription, mostly from the lower classes — an indication that Buddhism in Japan has some vitality still. On the front of the temple I saw a huge coil of rope as large as the hawser of a ship, made entirely of human hair, which had been cut off by numberless women and given to make this strand. I visited also Nishi Hongwanji, the headquarters of the particular sect of Buddhists for whom the temple is reared. Its buildings are solid and substantially constructed, and the interior is expensively and elaborately decorated. A big umbrella-like tree in one of the courtyards is supposed to be a protection against fire; and according to popular superstition, in case the temple should become ignited, this tree would discharge water on the fire, wherever it might be, in sufficient quantity to extinguish the flames.

I paid another visit to manufactories of porcelain, cloisonné, and iron. The iron work inlaid with gold is particularly beautiful.

I met wending its way through the streets a funeral procession which interested me greatly. In separate jinrikishas came first two Buddhist

Japanese vender of vegetables.

priests dressed in handsome robes and with their shaved heads bare. The body of the deceased, in a sitting posture, was enclosed in a lacquered open-work box carried on poles supported by the shoulders of two coolies. Following were the family and friends who accompanied the body to the place where it was cremated.

This incident suggested a visit to the crematory, which I made in the afternoon. It was near the top of a high hill, some distance from the town, in a beautiful spot entirely surrounded by a growth of small trees. Here were a temple and a large white building containing about a dozen brick ovens — if I may be allowed to call them so — as receptacles for the bodies. Iron doors are attached at either end. The fuel is put in position under the grating that holds the corpse, and also at each end, and surrounding it is placed cord-wood. The fire is then lighted and kept burning vigorously for six hours, when the bones and ashes that remain are removed by relatives and deposited in the cemetery. Everything about the crematory was in good condition, and the attendants were well-behaved. On my way home I purchased some seeds of the mammoth turnips so much cultivated in Japan, and sent them to Colonel J. Lion Gardiner, of Gardiner's Island, that he might try them on American soil.

On Friday morning, November 27th, I found on my way to the bath, which was at some distance from my hotel, that there had been a considerable fall in the temperature, and thin ice had formed. The day was fine, and I decided to go by jinrikisha to Lake Biwa. Setting out about nine o'clock, with two men each, we arrived at the Minarai-tei Hotel at Otsu at 10.30, in a snow flurry. This soon passed over, and I then proceeded down the shore of the lake to Karasaki, to see the mammoth sacred pine. This enormous tree is said to be two thousand years old, and is probably the largest and most curious tree of its species in existence. It is on a beautiful point of land jutting out into the lake, about three miles from Otsu. The branches are held up on a sort of scaffolding of wood and stone, and some of them trail near the ground in an oversweep of nearly three hundred feet.

The view from the obelisk at the Temple of Miidera, with the town below, the silvery lake, and the mountain for a background, is a harmonious and peculiarly lovely picture. Ishiyama-dera, a famous monastery, is also an interesting spot from which to obtain another fine view of Lake Biwa.

After this sight-seeing I went back to the hotel, and after tiffin returned to Kioto in time for dinner, with one more agreeable day in my

The temple grounds, Nara.

records. Saturday morning I left Kioto by train, arriving at Osaka about noon, and went at once to the Jiutei Hotel, which is pleasantly situated on the river bank and is kept in semi-European fashion. Here I had tiffin, and then went out with Ohashi in a jinrikisha to explore the town.

Tame deer at Nara.

Osaka is on the Yodogawa River and is intersected by numerous canals, which give it somewhat the appearance of Amsterdam. I visited the mint and several temples, and from the pagoda at one of them—the Tennōji—had a fine view of the city. At this temple also may be seen the curious praying machine—small wooden wheels, each revolution of which counts as a prayer.

We passed the castle grounds, enclosed by a moat and a high stone wall. The castle, which was burned in 1868, is said to have been the finest building in all Japan. Opposite are extensive barracks. We then went through several important business streets, which were filled in one instance with jugglery and other shows, and in another with handsome theatres and excellent shops.

On Sunday morning, November 29th, at 8.30, we took the train for Nara. I found this to be an exceptionally beautiful place. Arriving at about 10.30, we took jinrikishas and went first to the Kusuga-nō-Miyā temple. On the way we passed many shops containing the specialties of the place—India ink, toys, and sword-canes. On entering the temple grounds, which form a beautiful park, I was surprised to find great numbers of deer; their perfect tameness was shown in the little roadside stands where cakes are sold for feeding these pets. I halted and bought some of the cakes for a few cents, and immediately a dozen deer gathered about me to be fed.

The approach to the temple was lined with lanterns too numerous to count. We stopped first at the house where the *kagura*, an ancient dance, is performed by young girls. Their costume comprised red pantaloons and a white mantle. The hair was arranged in long pigtails, and a curious headdress of artificial flowers was worn on their foreheads. Their faces were covered with a thick coating of white powder. The girls while dancing held first a fan and afterward a stick with bells attached. Two priests and an old woman supplied the musical accompaniment, one priest singing and the other playing on a flute, while the old woman joined them on a kind of harp.

I then visited the Ni-gwatsn-dō temple, where there are more lanterns; but here they are all made of brass. The object that most interested me was the sacred white albino pony, standing in his little stable. Some beans were on sale near by, for the satisfaction of any one who wished to bestow a gratuity on the pony, and I bought a quantity and fed them to him. Like Captain Jinks's horse, he seemed accustomed to that fare. I then went to see the Daibutsu or enormous statue of Buddha, which is larger than the one at Kama-Kura, but is not considered so fine. This image is under cover in a temple, one part of which is arranged as a sort of museum, containing many images of hideous heathen gods. I then walked up Mikasa-yama, whence I had a magnificent view of the surrounding country. There are many cherry trees,

Head of god in Daibutsu temple, Nara.

which look remarkably fine when in blossom in the spring. These do not bear a good variety of cherry, however, the fruit being small and unfit for food. Many fine camphor trees surround the temples. We went to a pleasant little hotel and had our tiffin, which we had brought with us. Returning then to Nara and its hotel, I collected my luggage and proceeded to the station, and boarded the train for Kōbe, where I arrived at 8 P. M., and went to the Hôtel des Colonies.

Monday, November 30th, was warm and springlike. I spent the morning in looking at the town and in going on board the Verona, of the Peninsular and Oriental line, on which I was to embark the next day. There are many handsome foreign residences in Kōbe, and it is a rival of Yokohama in commercial affairs. In the afternoon, in company with Ohashi, my guide, I took a long jinrikisha ride, first to Nunōbiki waterfalls. There are two of these falls, one called the "male fall" and the other the "female fall," from their use as bathing places by the two

Nunobiki fall, Kōbe.

sexes. Skirting then the range of hills back of Kōbe, we went on until we reached Hiōgo, the town adjoining Kōbe. Returning along the water, we had a near view of the ships at anchor—the innumerable Japanese junks and sampans.

In Kōbe my attention was called to two curious facts. In Japan mirrors are made of bronze overlaid with highly polished tin and quicksilver. The bronze is usually handsomely ornamented with designs in *rilievo*, and "sunlight reflected from their face displays a luminous image of the design of their back." This peculiarity is produced by the method used in polishing the mirror. The other matter is the remarkable Japanese superstition in regard to foxes. The Japanese believe that a fox may enter a person's body and bewitch him, and there remain, unless by some means exorcised.

On Thursday, December 3d, in the morning, I amused myself walking about Kōbe, looking at the shops, going to the club, and visiting a saké distillery some little distance out of town. At four o'clock I went on board the steamship Verona, Captain F. H. Seymour, and at five o'clock we sailed for Nagasaki and Hong-Kong. I have never so much regretted leaving any country, so kindly disposed, refined, and polite are the Japanese, and so pleasant do they make the traveller's stay. On the

Bronze idol at Hiogo.

ship I met several of my fellow-passengers of the Empress of India. I had a fairly good cabin in the middle of the ship, but the Verona has a rather shabby, worn-out appearance compared with an Atlantic liner.

On Wednesday morning I got up before daylight, in order to be on deck as the steamer went through the Narrows between Oshima and Shikoku, where the passage is less than a hundred yards in width, with a rapid boiling current.

The day was lovely, warm, and sunny, the sea as smooth as a mirror, and in all directions junks and fishing-boats were to be seen. At twelve o'clock we passed through the fortified straits of Shimonoseki. The channel is well marked by lights and buoys, for the lighthouse system of Japan is equal to any in the world. The shores on both sides were dotted with villages and hamlets, and the whole effect was picturesque.

It took about one hour to go through the straits and into the open sea. The remainder of the day we skirted the coast, arriving at Nagasaki at twelve o'clock that night. In the lowering of the boat, one of the sailors, a Chinaman, fell overboard and was drowned. Thursday morning I woke up to find myself in the beautiful harbour of Nagasaki. It is perfectly landlocked, and, though much smaller, is not unlike the Golden Gate at San Francisco. The entrance is about a quarter of a mile wide.

On one side of the channel is the island of Pappenberg, from the cliffs of which, three hundred years ago, many thousands of Japanese Christians were thrown down and killed because they would not renounce their religion.

After breakfast I took a gondola-like sampan and went ashore, as the Verona was to occupy the day in coaling. I went first to pay my respects to the American consul, Dr. Abercrombie, but unfortunately he was absent at Shanghai. I had the opportunity, though, of seeing some American newspapers, just arrived. The American consulate is beautifully situated, overlooking the town, and surrounded by a terraced garden filled with orange, banana, and camellia trees. The person in charge of the office, a Portuguese, treated me with much politeness, which a traveller always appreciates when he visits the representative of his country in a foreign land.

I then took a jinrikisha and visited a number of shops, where beautifully carved tortoise shell is sold at very low prices. On my way to the Belle-Vue Hotel—a French establishment where I took tiffin—I stopped at the Osuwa Temple to see the famous bronze horse that stands in the courtyard, and noticed that in Nagasaki, as elsewhere in

Japan, there are large numbers of cats. But these differ from the common cat of America and Europe, in having a short tail something like that of a rabbit. After tiffin I went on board the Verona again, and at 5 P. M. we set sail for Hong-Kong.

In every respect my visit to Japan was successful. I can even say, as very few travellers can, that I had but one rainy day while travelling through the " Land of the Rising Sun."

Japanese girls.

CHAPTER V.

VISIT TO CHINA.

LEAVING Nagasaki harbour on Thursday afternoon, December 3d, we were soon admonished that a terrific gale was blowing outside. It increased, too, and the ensuing night was the most uncomfortable that I have ever spent at sea. The Verona rolled so that I could hardly keep myself in my berth, even by holding on with both hands. Sleep, of course, was impossible, especially as the sea had broken in one of the skylights on deck, and torrents of water were rushing through the passage in front of my door. At one time the captain hove the ship to, as it was impossible to proceed. The gale continued for about thirty hours, after which it gradually subsided, and by Saturday morning the water was quite smooth again.

Mr. James A. Melville, of Edinburgh, Scotland, whom I had first met at Vancouver, and afterward frequently in Japan, I found a most intelligent and agreeable companion. He and Dr. Barbour were on a commission, upon which they had been sent by the Free Church of Scotland, to examine the missionary fields in Amoy, China, and Formosa, and to report upon them. Mr. Melville also undertook the task of writing letters on his travels to the Edinburgh Scotsman, the Montreal Star, and the Melbourne Argus. These letters were most clever productions.

On Saturday the water was smooth and the air warm and pleasant. The spirits of the passengers by dinner-time had fairly revived, and they were beginning to forget their awful experience of the day before. Sunday, December 6th, the weather continued good, and in the morning we sighted land. It was our first view of the Celestial Empire. We were passing through the channel separating the island of Formosa from the mainland, and the sea remained smooth although we were running before the monsoon, which was blowing hard.

Monday morning, going on deck, I found we were passing a curious peak-shaped rock directly in the channel, which was without lighthouse or bell to warn mariners in a fog of its existence. The captain said it was the terror of navigators in these waters. Its distance from Hong-Kong is only fifty-four miles, and it is surprising that no beacon has been placed there.

The coast of China was plainly discernible, the shore being a succession of sharp-pointed hills. Numerous fishing-junks were busy in all directions. They are quite different from the Japanese boats, and are built so as to trim very low at the bow. The sail is usually made of matting.

Hong-Kong, which means "Fragrant Stream," is an island about eleven miles long and from two to five miles broad, and has an excellent harbour, which presents an animated appearance. It is a British colony with a garrison, and the red coat of Tommy Atkins adds to the picturesqueness of the streets. The police are all tall, dark-skinned Sikhs, dressed in blue coats and red turbans and carrying clubs. They are brought here from India to act in their constabulary capacity. The

Joss-house, Hong-Kong

city is officially known as Victoria, although the name is seldom used in ordinary parlance. It is magnificently situated, the houses, which are large and solid, rising tier upon tier to the top of the hill.

Victoria Peak, above the town, commands a splendid prospect. At 1 P. M. the Verona made fast to her buoy, and shortly afterward we were transported to the *praya* or quay in a steam launch, and went at once to the Hong-Kong Hotel. It was difficult for me to realize that I was indeed in Far Cathay. Here, to my great delight, I found

letters from home, which I read with avidity. Having written my replies so that they might go in the steamer sailing on the morrow for Vancouver, I began to make inquiries. I learned that the hurricane we encountered at sea had swept over Hong-Hong, destroying several ships and about three hundred sampans and junks, and causing the death of nearly a thousand Chinamen. These hurricanes and typhoons are of frequent occurrence, and at times produce awful calamities.

At 5 P.M. I took a jinrikisha to the steamboat Fatshan, bound for Canton. This boat was built of steel, at Leith, Scotland, on the plan of a Long Island Sound steamboat, and is a splendid craft. We entered the Canton or Pearl River at 5.30; the air was balmy, and the sun was setting in a golden cloud, which made the prospect most beautiful.

It seems that the pigtail that is worn universally by all classes of Chinamen is a token of subjection to the Emperor Kwang-Hsu. When the present dynasty, the Ta-Tsing, which is Tartar, came into power by conquest in 1644, it decreed that all the men of the country, of whatever degree or rank, should wear the pigtail to show their loyalty; and this custom has been continued ever since. In some localities the Roman Catholic monks and priests, with strange inconsistency, have adopted the costume of the country and also the pigtail, thinking thereby to get the good will and confidence of the Chinese. But this has not prevented attacks upon them; indeed, it has made them more odious to some of the natives. The Protestant missionaries of the China Inland Mission have also adopted the native dress.

English-speaking people use pigeon English—a sort of mixture of English, Portuguese, and Chinese—almost entirely, in communicating with the lower classes at Hong-Kong. Some of the phrases are quite extraordinary; for instance, the lord bishop is designated as " Number One topside heaven pigeon man." " Missa Craigie gottee one piecee small cow chile " conveys the information that Mrs. Craigie has presented her husband with a daughter.

The Chinese women of the higher classes, although they do not cover their faces like the women of Turkey, will not permit themselves to be seen in public, always going about in closed palanquins. In fact, one sees but few of the women with the small feet; for in China women of the poorest and lowest caste have feet of the natural size, and they, of course, are the ones most seen.

On Tuesday, December 8th, we arrived at Canton at 6.30 A. M. Such a sight I could never have imagined as presented itself when I went on deck. The water was covered with boats of all sizes. In the

Foreign buildings on Sha-Mien Island, Canton.

middle of the stream were Chinese gunboats—some built in European style, others the old-fashioned junks—an American man-of-war, and many foreign merchant ships, while on the sides of the river was a swarm of sampans. Several hundred thousand of the population of Canton live in these boats. For generations Chinese have been born, have lived, and have died on a sampan—a feature of life that can hardly be found elsewhere. Soon after breakfast I engaged Ah Cum, Jr., as guide, and we set out in chairs to see the town, each with three coolies. The streets are very narrow, the widest not being more than ten feet from house to house.

The houses are substantially built of brick and stone, and the streets are paved with long slabs of granite. We first visited factories where embroidery and ivory carving were done, where jewellery was fashioned of silver inlaid with the feathers of the kingfisher, and where jade cutting was artistically executed. We then proceeded to the temple of the five hundred Buddhas. This was not especially noticeable after those of Japan, but I was interested to see the image of Marco Polo pointed out among the five hundred. Of another Buddha the gilding was all worn off the belly, the result of its being rubbed by women unable to bear children, who hoped to propitiate the gods, that their curse, as they consider it, might be removed.

We then stopped at a butcher's shop that dealt exclusively in the flesh of cats, dogs, and rats, which the lower classes eat with seeming relish. A black cat or dog brings a much higher price than one of another colour, as its meat is considered more nourishing. Along the narrow streets we met several horrible lepers.

The next place we visited was the spot, near a pottery, where criminals are beheaded. The ground was covered with blood from some recent executions, and in several stone jars were the heads of the culprits. We also saw the crosses still used to crucify the condemned, who, when crucified, are sliced up with sharp knives. For a small sum the beheading sword was brought out and shown.

Thence we went to the Summer Palace, in one of the rooms of

which I had my tiffin, which I had brought with me. After a suitable rest we repaired to the "five-story pagoda," so called, although it is not a pagoda but a sort of lookout set on the city wall; for it must be noted that Canton is a walled town, defended with curious rusty old cannon, and has sixteen gates. The view from the pagoda is fine.

Chinese Tomb, Canton.

We next visited the Hall of Examination, which has eleven thousand six hundred and sixteen little cells, where students compete triennially for one hundred and thirty positions of the second literary degree. The test, as one can understand, is terribly severe.

Pursuing our way still further, we visited the city of the dead, where bodies are kept embalmed until their final resting place is prepared. Here dozens of brick rooms are arranged as shrines or small temples, and behind a curtain is the huge coffin containing the corpse

The five-story Pagoda, Canton.

of some mandarin or his wife or his children. A cup of tea is always there, and a few fresh flowers.

We then passed on to the flowery or nine-story pagoda (this must not be confounded with the "flowery boats" which at night, when lighted, present such a gay appearance, and which are the habitation of the frail women of Canton), and thence went to the mosque—for a large number of Chinamen are followers of Mahomet. Going to the prisons, we saw first that of the ordinary thieves and vagabonds, who wear around their necks a square piece of board with a central hole. The board is opened for the passage of the head, and is then closed for the term of the culprit's sentence. This is a terribly uncomfortable thing to sleep with, but I believe the unfortunates get accustomed to it. The other prisoners—murderers and pirates—seemed to have an easier time, as they only wore shackles on their feet. We stopped next to see the famous water clock, as it is called, but I found it nothing but a row of four iron tubs, from one to another of which the water dribbles within a certain time, after the manner of sand in an hourglass.

To finish the day's sights, I went to the Temple of Confucius and the Honam Temple, where I viewed the Holy Pigpen containing the sacred swine. These animals looked and acted very much like the original hog, and were certainly no cleaner in their habits than their less sanctified brethren. One object not to be forgotten was the Temple of Horrors. Here are small wooden figures arranged to represent the following scenes:

West Side.	East Side.
1. Transmigration.	1. Sawing a man between boards.
2. Grinding a culprit.	2. Transmigration.
3. Boiling in oil.	3. Bastinado.
4. Under the red-hot bell.	4. Trial of a criminal.
5. Beheading.	

After four o'clock tea at the Shameen Hotel, on the foreign concession, I returned in a sampan to our steamboat, the Fatshan, in order to return to Hong-Kong at 5 P.M. The sampan was managed by three girls, and it was wonderful with what skill they worked their way through the confused mass of boats of all descriptions and sizes. I was glad to have seen Canton, yet it was an experience that one would not wish to repeat very soon.

As we passed down the river we found the prominence and size of the French Roman Catholic cathedral very striking. It is the most noticeable object in the approach to Canton or in leaving it. I am told that there are a considerable number of Catholics there, but many people doubt the sincerity of Chinese Christians, who are said to demand a small salary to remain converted.

I sat on deck until it was almost dark, interested in the varying scenes presented, rice paddies, high hills, fields of grain, etc. Finally the bell sounded for dinner, a meal I fully appreciated on that occasion, and soon after it I went to bed, tired but well satisfied with my day in a Chinese city.

On Wednesday morning the vessel arrived bright and early at Hong-Kong; I took a chair to the Hong-Kong Hotel, and secured a good room facing the Queen's Road. After breakfast I went to the Public Gardens, and saw a large India-rubber tree for the first time; thence, by the Bowen Road, to the Happy Valley, where the race-course and the Parsee and the English cemeteries are, returning by the Queen's Road, east. The scenery along the whole route was superb. Bowen Road, like all other roads on the Peak, is excellently built; in many places it is walled up, and in others fenced for long distances with iron railings. The race-course in Happy Valley is a remarkably level spot, surrounded by high hills rising abruptly. I should think the meetings would be the most picturesque of any under the Union Jack. The English and the Parsees, or followers of Zoroaster, have adjoining cemeteries, both of which are exceptionally beautiful. Most of those buried in the English ground were soldiers and sailors serving their country on this station.

On my return through the town I passed the barracks, where the

Racecourse in Happy Valley, Hong-Kong.
(Circuit about seven eighths of a mile.)

Argyle and Sutherland Highlanders were stationed. In their uniform of white short tunics and kilts and white helmet they look better than when wearing the full-dress red coat. Hong-Kong is a well-arranged and well-ordered city; those in authority have understood how to transform a barren, rocky island into a handsome town with beautiful suburbs. How often in the United States is the reverse the case!

The Governor at Home, Hong-Kong.

How often are places that nature has made beautiful marred by the hands of vulgarity and ignorance in control!

Returning for tiffin, I spent a little time in shopping, and then took the tramway to the Peak, which rises eighteen hundred feet above the city of Victoria. It is ascended by a railway, worked by a stationary engine after the fashion of those on the Rigi and Mount Pilatus. On attaining the summit, I discovered, to my surprise, that there were splendid villas and huge hotels upon it, all built in the most expensive and substantial manner. I found also plenty of coolies waiting with chairs for the accommodation of passengers.

I made my way to a point of observation above the Austin Hotel, and there I spent two hours in looking at the marvellous picture spread before me. Far and wide the sea was visible, and the town and shipping had a toylike appearance that was very attractive. I do not think I have ever taken a birds'-eye view to better advantage. With regret I left this scene of enchantment, but the setting sun warned me that it was time to return.

Arriving at the end of the tramway, I walked back to town, and in passing the Anglican cathedral I could not but stop to admire the way in which seven Chinese lads were playing shuttlecock with their feet, the cock going in rotation up in the air from each one to the next. As I came down the tramway, I might add, I had an excellent view of the reservoir, and in the distance loomed up the splendid residence of Mr. Keswick, head of the firm of Jardine, Matheson & Co., the richest commercial house of China. The historical American house of Russell & Co. has ceased to exist. In former times it was all-powerful in Hong-Kong, and many young American gentlemen came out and made their fortunes in its employ. The methods of the house finally became obsolete and expensive, and after maintaining a precarious existence for some years, it finally succumbed last spring.

Besides the island of Hong-Kong, a small strip of land called Kowloon, on the opposite side of the harbour, belongs to the colony. Here many new buildings and wharves are in construction. This settlement adjoins the Chinese Kowloon, which is inhabited by a piratical population. At this Kowloon occur frequent executions, which many persons go over from Hong-Kong to witness. The prisoners to be executed are placed on their knees in a row, and the executioner is assisted by a man who holds up the culprit's queue, whereat with one stroke of the sword the head is completely severed from the body and drops on the ground, while the trunk falls over

Chinese criminals awaiting death.

it. It is considered to be painless, this death administered by the Chinese sword.

Thursday morning, December 10th, on looking out, I found the Queen's Road lined with Sikh policemen, and on inquiring I was told that the new governor of the colony, Sir William Robinson, would land from the steamship Empress of Japan at eleven o'clock. At that hour all was excitement; a guard of honour from the Argyle and Sutherland Highlanders was stationed at the landing-stage to receive the approaching executive as he reached the shore; the ships of war fired a salute, and the regimental band played the national anthem. A broad red carpet was spread for the governor's use in stepping from the launch to the shore. Being landed, he immediately took his seat in a handsome Sedan chair carried by a dozen coolies habited in red blouses and hats with a long red tassel to each. He was followed by his family in other chairs and by the representatives of the civil and military authorities, in full uniform, and passed rapidly through the town on his way to the Government House farther up the Peak.

As soon as the military had disappeared I went on board the tender and was conveyed to the Rosetta, thirty-five hundred tons, Captain C. Gadd, of the Peninsular and Oriental line. It was pleasant to find that the stewards were English, for since visiting China I had taken a dislike to the Chinese. The sailors, who were nearly all lascars, wore a picturesque dress of white cotton with red turban. Among the passengers were eight Parsees returning to Bombay. At one o'clock the engines began to move, and soon we had passed out into the China Sea and were running before a light monsoon. I noticed a Chinaman on board with a long white moustache, an unusual sight, and was informed that this appendage showed him to be a grandfather.

Although the sea was comparatively smooth, our ship had considerable motion, and I found that she was dubbed by the sailors the Rolling Rose. On Friday came a noticeable change in the temperature, the air growing so warm and oppressive that at dinner the punkahs were set in motion.

The Chinese generally travel by boat, as the kingdom is intersected by water-ways. Where the natural channels fail, a canal is dug to piece out the highway. They care nothing about speed—time seems of no account—but their boats have clean and comfortable cabins. The junks

Chinese pagoda, Canton, five thousand nine hundred years old.

of the officials are like floating homes. They are fitted with what a Chinaman would call every convenience, and have a small army of rowers and polers and towers. The flag of the mandarin floats at every masthead. These junks have no sail except one that can be lifted when the wind is direct aft, but the travelling boats of the common people carry much sail, and the seamen are expert in its use. They are also more easily towed, as they are lighter in construction. They have a movable deck, and the crew sleep in the place made by removing it. The sea-going junks are large, high at both ends, and square at bow and stern. On the stern is painted a phœnix, standing on a rock in midocean, and at the bows are the two great, wide-open eyes. The pigeon-English explanation of the eyes is, "No have got eye, how can see? No can see, how can savey?" The vessels have water-tight compartments, and carry thousands of tons of cargo. They are three-masted. The sails are all made of matting. The Chinese spend as much thought,

After the execution.

with a great deal more ingenuity and success, upon names for their craft as a New York travelling van. Columbus never could have originated in China; for to this day they hug the shore because they don't know how to take observations or trust solely to the compass. As a consequence, there is much destruction of boats and of the lives of sailors. The loss is the greater because of the multitudes of people who live all the year round on junks, and of the typhoons that sweep over the water. The population that inhabit the boats are not Chinese proper, but descendants of an earlier race. The Cantonese do not allow them to compete at their schools, or marry their children, and persecutions are frequent, of the "water-fowl," as they are contemptuously called. Meantime, regardless of the light in which it is looked upon, a *tanka*, or "water-fowl" baby lies on the deck of its father's junk with only an empty gourd tied between its shoulders to keep it afloat a while if it tumbles overboard.

This method of getting about by water must save the native a great deal of discomfort, for the roads in China are of the roughest, and are never mended. The carts have no springs, and the passenger sits cross-legged. Mules are generally preferred to horses, and oxen are often employed to draw private carriages. The horse is an importation into China; the ancient hieroglyphic used for its name was originally made to represent a donkey. The wheelbarrow is a common vehicle, especially in northern China. It is propelled by men or by one man, who often pushes two people, his toil assisted by a sail, which is moved about with the wind. The wheel is placed under the barrow. Human beings carry tremendous loads in their carts, so cheap is such labour compared with that of animals. But even in China the locomotive is beginning to be the burden-carrier. Where the once magnificent but now neglected highways run, there is much ancient work that could be made to assist the engineer.

Another reason why a traveller who would study the customs of China would prefer to travel as much as possible by water is that the inns are terribly dirty and uncomfortable, while on the boat a stove is carried so that his food can be cooked and served in his decent cabin or on deck. If the traveller wishes to live as the Chinese do, he must begin by learning to use the chop-stick, although it seems so evident that he would be compelled to starve before this was accomplished that the officials and others who entertain "foreign devils" give them knives and forks. Mutton, pork, beef, goat, ducks, wild and domestic fowl, and even game, are used; but either these are dear, or the taste of the people is very degenerate, for the more common diet is far less appetizing. In Canton, the poulterers keep dried rats, which sell readily because they are liked, and also because they cure baldness, although how a shaven-headed people find that out it is not easy to tell. Horse flesh is also sold openly, and there are dog and cat restaurants. These meats are fried with water chestnuts and the universal garlic and oil. Placards sometimes announce to the hurried passer —if there is such a being in China—that a slice of black cat or black dog can be had at a moment's notice. The colour makes them especially nourishing. On a particular day in the opening of the hot season, dog's meat is eaten to make the eater impervious to heat and disease. Dog hams are a luxury only attainable by the rich. Of course rice is the one universal diet, although it is absent from the table just in proportion to the ability of the individual to buy meat or fish. Frogs form a common dish among the poor, and locusts and grasshoppers are eaten. The former are fried in the street and vended from the curbstone. Fish of all kinds are relished. Both nets and lines are used in catching them. The cormorant is used as a fisher in inland lakes. The rower takes his raft to a quiet place, ties a string loosely around the bird, pushes it off into the water, and when it rises with its prey, throws a landing net over both. Fish-breeding is carried on extensively. Oysters and mussels are eaten. The mussels are often caught, tiny images of Buddha forced into their shells, and thrown back into the pool, to be taken out later covered with mother-of-pearl. The contrasted bills of fare of a Canton restaurant and a Chinese gentleman's dinner for guests will be interesting.

Public garden, Hong-Kong.

The following is from a bill of fare presented at a restaurant:

Cat's flesh, one basin, 10 cents.   Ketchup, one basin, 3 cash.
Wine, one bottle, 3 cents.   Black dog's grease, 1 tael, 4 cents.
Wine, one small bottle, 1 cent.   Black cat's eyes, one pair, 4 cents.
Congee, one basin, 2 cash.

All guests dining at this restaurant are requested to be punctual in their payments.

The dinner given by the gentleman consisted of these dishes, served in courses:

Sharks' fins, with crab sauce.   Fried slices of pheasant.
Pigeons' eggs stewed with mushrooms.   Mushroom broth.
Sliced sea-slugs in chicken broth, with   *Dessert.*
  ham.   Two dishes of fried pudding—one
Wild duck with Shan-Toong cabbage.   sweet, the other salt.
Fried fish.   Sweetened duck.
Lumps of pork fat fried in rice flour.   Strips of boned chicken fried in oil.
Stewed lily roots.   Boiled fish with soy.
Chicken mashed to pulp with ham.   Lumps of parboiled mutton, fried in
Stewed bamboo shoots.   pork fat.
Stewed shellfish.

As in everything else, the Chinese are most provident in the care of their fish and other food preserves, which makes it seem all the more strange that they make no use whatever of the milk of cows.

The appearance of a Chinese city, seen either in approaching or in leaving it, is that of houses having almost the same height and construction, and only the pagodas and palaces give variety. The pagodas are generally built of brick, and are five, seven, and nine or more stories high always an uneven number. The walls are double, and between them wind the staircases that lead to the summit. At each story are doorways. The outer wall is octagonal, and broken by the projecting roofs of tiles that form the cover of each story. They are turned up at the corners, and hung with bells. The Buddhist pagodas are the oldest structures in China, but the remarkable thing about Chinese architecture is its comparative frailty. Old as are the traditions which they are intended to perpetuate, the tentlike form and delicate fabric forbid them to survive any great lapse of time. The Confucian temples are similar in structure to those built for relics of Buddha or for the remains of his priests and noble worshippers. The law compels every city and market town in the empire to have at least one of these temples, and insists that it shall have three courtyards, one behind the other, all opening to the south.

There is a semicircular pond in the lower end of the courtyard, which has a bridge across it, but it is never crossed except by the emperor and the *chewaugh yuens* —those who have won that highest title by success at the competitive examinations. For them the southern wall is pierced by a gateway, which they only can enter. Every city in China has a wall around it, on which are fortified towers and battlements. The roofs of the houses, which are the most

Private residence and grounds, Hong-Kong.

ornamental part, have a bright appearance from the colouring of the tiles. Only the houses of certain classes are allowed to have glazed tiles, and yellow is a favourite colour for them. But as fashion dictates that the houses of the rich and well-to-do shall have a high wall surrounding them, and that no window shall look outward, the stretch of brick is only broken by front doors, which are kept scrupulously closed. Screens stand inside, at a little distance, to protect the interior in case necessity or carelessness causes the gate to be left open. Behind the screen is a courtyard, on either side of which are the rooms occupied by the servants. A passage, reached by a few steps, leads to an inner courtyard, around which are the family rooms, still another passage being used by servants and tradesmen. There is little knowledge of what goes to make comfort in the fittings of a Chinese house. The only protection against cold is clothing, garments being added until their weight prohibits motion. The furniture is of wood, of angular shape, sometimes with a few hard cushions. The beds are little better, with their oblong cubes of bamboo for pillows. On this structure a woman must arrange her head so as not to disturb a single one of the hairs that are elaborately dressed with bandoline, and intended to keep their fantastic arrangement for days at a time. Each Chinese province has its method of hair-dressing. In Canton the ordinary style is to have the back hair plastered into the semblance of a teapot handle, while the sides are ornamented with pins and flowers, natural or artificial. The bang is worn only by the unmarried. The time of change from winter to summer dress and the reverse is decided upon by an edict from the emperor. A Chinese lady plasters her complexion, paints her lips, trims her eyebrows, and otherwise disfigures herself; but there is no folly that resembles tight lacing and hooped petticoats until we come to the cruelty practised upon the feet. A working woman of the Hakkas class has something left to stand upon. But the wife of a well-to-do Chinaman is almost as helpless as when she was born. At five years old the girl baby's feet are bound with the four smaller toes bent under the foot and the instep forced upward and backward. High-heeled shoes are put on, and in time the woman has two pegs at the end of shrivelled lower limbs. What do the Darwinians say to the fact that Chinese babies are still born with the pretty shapely foot of a distant ancestress? The Manchoos and the Hakkas of Canton are exceptions to the otherwise universal practice. The queue worn by the man is as unnatural a disfigurement, although not so cruel or harmful. The first ruler of the present dynasty compelled the conquered nation to be shaved with the exception of the crown. Into the hair that is allowed to grow are woven various materials, according to the owner's wealth, to form the pigtail, which, at length, has come to be looked upon as a glory rather than a shame among those not in open rebellion.

Marriage in China is attended, as are all their rites, with vast ceremony. Generally the young people have never seen each other, as etiquette permits no acquaintance between youths and maidens, the wedding being arranged by third parties. When, at last, after many preliminaries, the bridegroom stands in the reception-room on a dais, the bride comes and prostrates herself at his feet. He descends to her side and, raising her veil, gazes on her for the first time. Then they sit down in silence, each one trying to sit on the garments of the other, as the one who succeeds will be ruler of the house. After many ceremonies, during which the bridegroom eats and the bride refuses the offered food, she sits answering riddles late into the night or otherwise entertains her guests alone, for custom forbids that husband and wife should ever be seen in public together. Divorce is easy for the husband, impossible for the wife, and suicide to escape marriage is not at all uncommon. Life is cheaply held, and such is the honour bestowed on those who have the courage to take their own lives, that the widow who voluntarily dies at her husband's tomb is given a foretaste of the fame that is to crown her name. It is considered of the greatest importance that the whole family be present at the deathbed of a Chinese householder. His last words are noted, and he is placed in the main hall to die. Here his body is prepared for burial, many precious things

Queen's Road Central, Hong-Kong.

being placed in the coffin, and a Sedan chair being burned, that its spirit may transport his in the other world. The ceremonies of mourning continue for many months, and the greatest importance is attached to them. So necessary is it to find exactly the proper site for the tomb that the burial is sometimes delayed for years while an expert is searching, compass in hand, up and down the land. Then a lucky day must be found for the interment. As the things that render days unlucky for such purpose are numerous, delays are frequent. Should any relative of the deceased be *enceinte*, there could be no funeral until after the birth. The eldest son follows the body of his father, leaning upon a bamboo staff to show overwhelming sorrow, while for his mother he leans upon a cane of *t'ung*, to show that the grief is not inconsolable.

The English Church at Canton

Penang Harbour.

CHAPTER VI.

THROUGH THE STRAITS TO CEYLON.

ON Saturday, December 12th, the weather continued to grow warmer, and we were in sight of the coast of Siam for several hours, but not near enough to see the character of the country. The sea was smooth, being protected eastward by the Philippine Islands and Borneo. During the afternoon we were off the mouth of Cambodia River.

On Sunday we were again favoured with a delightful tropical day. Divine service was heard on deck, the captain reading the prayers *en grande tenue*, and all the officers being present in their neat white duck uniform. The reading-desk was covered with the Union Jack, and a volunteer choir gave the music, with piano and violin accompaniment. At 1.20 the observation showed us to be

A Ceylon elephant.

crossing the Gulf of Siam. The evening was ideal, a moon nearly full shining brightly on the placid sea.

Monday was another pleasant day. In the afternoon tea was served on deck, after which we had an amateur concert, consisting of vocal and instrumental music, the latter on the violin, the piano, and the zither. Tuesday morning we were nearing Singapore. The ship passed the city and continued for three miles to the wharves, which are on a little island connected with the larger one. We were soon made fast, and at once I left the ship and took a *gharry*, a curious sort of cab, drawn by a strong little Malay pony about twelve hands high, driven by a *kling*. It is surprising what a heavy load these ponies will draw and how fast they can go.

The superiority of the European race—in size as well as intelligence—to the other races is very marked on Eastern ground. I was struck with this fact before we landed at the wharf, where a group of perhaps a dozen Englishmen were waiting to come on board. They were dressed after the European manner there, in spotless white, and the contrast to the motley crowd of natives was strongly presented.

After a three-mile drive I arrived at the Hôtel de l'Europe, at which I had expected to find a Cingalese guide who had been recommended to me for Ceylon and India. I had written to him to be ready, and he had gone to the steamer, where I had missed him. Soon, however, Pereira—for that was his name—made his appearance, and informed me that he was in the employ of the Malay Government, keeping a "rest-house," or hotel, and was under contract for two years—a contract impossible for him to break. He had come up expressly to see me from his station, which was two days distant by steamer. This was a touching piece of devotion, I thought; but afterward I found that I was expected to pay his way up and back, besides showing my appreciation of this concern in a substantial present. However, as he immediately took charge of me and addressed me in every sentence as "Master," it would have been most ungracious to begrudge the cost.

Fortunately, the day was overcast, so I amused myself by driving around the town, visiting the Museum, the Botanical Gardens, and many excellent shops. The bungalows where the foreigners live are mostly beautiful and attractive villas. The roads are as hard as a floor, and the lawns as fine as any in England. This, of course, is

Tiger-shooting in the Malay peninsula.

owing to the moist atmosphere and the frequent rains. The tropical trees and flowers grow in a most luxuriant manner.

On the island of Singapore, even at the present time, tigers are frequently killed in the jungle. Twenty years ago they were very destructive to human life, one person a day being the average killed and eaten by these ferocious beasts. Singapore has a population of about 140,000 souls, and is the capital of what are known as the "Straits Settlements," which consist of Singapore, Penang, and Ma-

The Sultan of Johor's palace, near Singapore.

lacca, or Wellesley. It is neighbour to Java, Borneo, and Sumatra. The island of Singapore proper is twenty-seven miles long by fourteen miles wide, and is separated by a channel three fourths of a mile wide from the dominion and the palace of the Sultan of Johore. The Sultan is thoroughly Europeanized in his ways, and spends most of his time in London and Paris. I had met him at Homburg, and it had been my intention to drive out to his palace to pay my respects to him, but I learned that he was then absent, so I did not go. He is said to entertain in most lavish style. To each guest, lady or gentleman, immediately on arrival a eunuch is assigned as a special servant. The eunuch sleeps on a mat in the guest's room, ready to be of service at any moment. The ladies, especially, find this feature a decided novelty.

Sir Stamford Raffles, who in about the second decade of the century married the daughter of the Rajah of Johore of that period, founded Singapore in 1819. At first it was under Indian rule, but in 1867 it was transferred by the Indian Government, and was made a crown colony.

The steamers of the various lines to Singapore go for the most part to the Tanjong Pagar wharf. The harbour of Singapore is crowded with shipping and British men-of-war. European trading-vessels, hundreds of Malay *proas* and Chinese junks, fishing-boats and passenger *sampans* make a lively scene. The government and troops of the town are English, as well as

A Dyak of Borneo.

the chief merchants. The mass of the population is Chinese—the wealthy merchants and large farmers, as well as the mechanics and labourers, being of that race. The native Malays are usually fishermen and boatmen, while they also supply the police force. The clerks and small merchants are mostly Portuguese of Malacca, while the grooms and washermen are all Bengalese. Many of the sailors are Japanese, and there is a sprinkling of Dyaks from Borneo and natives of other islands of the archipelago.

The architecture of the town shows the same variety. There are handsome public buildings and churches, Mohammedan mosques, Chinese joss-houses, fine European dwellings, huge substantial warehouses, quaint *kling* and Chinese bazars, and many streets of Chinese and Malay cottages.

The Sultan of Johore

In the twelfth century the city of Singapore (Lion's Town) occupied the site and was capital of a Malayan kingdom. It fell into decay, and when, in 1819, the British built a factory there, the whole island had but a hundred and fifty inhabitants. In 1824 the Sultan of Johore transferred the sovereignty of the island to the British, since which time its progress has been great. It is the natural *entrepôt* for the commerce of southern Asia and the Indian Archipelago, and is a free port. The largest vessels can drop anchor in its wide harbour.

The drays and carts that frequent the streets are drawn each by the active little Indian bullock with a large hump on his back. He travels along at a speed of four or five miles an hour. There was considerable excitement in Singapore on the 15th of December, as a circus had come to town—an unusual event at the Straits. The performance announced was the "Wild West, or Frontier Life in America."

At the Hôtel de l'Europe dinner was served under a colonnade open on one side to the air, and I then took a *gharry*, drove back to the Rosetta, and turned into my bunk for the night.

Nutmeg Plantation, Penang.

On Wednesday morning, December 16th, at eight o'clock, our steamer continued her trip through the Straits. The scene on the wharf just before our departure was very amusing. Many natives were there, with various articles to sell. Monkeys could be bought for two dollars a pair; beautiful little paroquets with a cage, for one dollar a pair; while Malacca canes—a bunch of a dozen—and fine specimens of coral and shells, could be had for a few cents. As the Rosetta began to move out into the stream a crowd of half-naked boys in canoes surrounded us, and the passengers threw into the water pieces of money, which the boys dived for, a sinking penny being overtaken and seized before it reached the bottom.

The weather continued pleasant, with an occasional shower. Land could be seen on both sides of the Straits, which were as smooth as any river. In the evening the moon shone full and bright, and many on board indulged in dancing and singing. These nights were so lovely that it was unusually late before we left the deck; in fact, some of the passengers brought up their beds and slept in the cool breeze in preference to keeping the stuffy cabins.

On Thursday, at one o'clock, we reached the port of Georgetown, Prince of Wales Island, commonly called Penang, from Pulo Penang or Betel-nut Island, as the native name signified. It is a beautiful spot, two miles off the Straits of Malacca, facing Deli, a Dutch colony in Sumatra. The island is twenty miles long by nine miles wide. On the Malay side is the province of Wellesley, two miles distant, on a strip of land thirty-five miles in breadth and eighty miles in length. The British purchased Penang in 1786, and Wellesley in 1800, from the Rajah of Quedah.

It is an interesting fact that one ship of Captain Kidd, the famous "pirate" (so called), was the Quedah Merchant, and she had been captured, with the dowry of the daughter of the Great Mogul on board, by Kidd's original vessel, the Adventure Galley.

I went ashore in a peculiarly shaped boat of sharp prow and broad stern, which was propelled by a man standing at the extreme end of the stern, with a pair of oars that were shaped like spades. On landing, I took a *gharry* and a guide, and drove first to the Oriental Hotel, which is delightfully situated directly on the water and is surrounded by a tropical garden. Hence we went through the town, which has a Portuguese or Spanish appearance. The population is composed of a variety of races and creeds, like that of Singapore.

The *kling* children look very funny here, walking about with no clothing whatever, but with a silver shield the size of a five-franc piece, hung around their bodies by a silver chain, and falling in front of the person so as not to shock European sensibilities. Sometimes they wear also, on their arms and ankles, bangles of silver, which contrast well with their dark skin.

There are pleasant-looking and handsome buildings on the island — the Penang Club, the Government House, and many of the bungalows of the foreign and Chinese merchants; for some of the latter are wealthy and have luxurious establishments, with their imported English horses and dog-carts in European style.

We drove out to the waterfall, a pretty cascade in a well-kept park, passing large groves of palms, principally the cocoanut and the sago, and bread-fruit and betel-nut trees. No oranges are cultivated here, it being too hot for them. The native houses are usually built on posts ten feet high—a construction that has many sanitary advantages, and makes a refuge from the aggressions of reptiles, noxious insects, and wild animals.

From both Singapore and Penang are shipped large quantities of tin, which is mined at Perak, a native state under a British protectorate on the Peninsula. I was informed that this business, as well as the tobacco trade, had been disturbed considerably by the new American tariff.

The temperature at the Straits of Malacca is the same the year round, the only difference being that there is more rain in certain months than in others; but there is great humidity of the air at

Temple at Penang.

all seasons, and this makes the heat more perceptible than in a like temperature of dry air, especially when one takes active exercise. The range of the thermometer daily is from 60° to 95° Fahrenheit.

Returning to the landing-stairs, I was conveyed to the ship by a steam launch kindly placed at my disposal by the governor. At 7

Siam Pagoda, Penang.

P. M. we hoisted anchor and sailed away, the full moon shining on the placid water. Later in the evening the beautiful constellation of the Southern Cross was pointed out to me. On Friday the heat was extremely oppressive. In the afternoon we passed in sight of Sumatra and the Dutch colony of Acheen. At dinner I ate for the first time a mangosteen, a fruit that grows at Penang. It is excellent in flavour, and different from any other fruit that I have seen.

On the Rosetta the passengers were about equally divided between Americans and English. The two nationalities, as a rule, do not understand each other and are not sympathetic. The English are undoubtedly very jealous of the wealth and power of the United States. The McKinley bill they consider as especially aimed at their manufactures, and they complain bitterly of its effect.

Elephant working at tannery, Pegu.

The officers of these Oriental lines of steamers spend much of their time in dancing and flirting with the ladies. This is not permitted on the Atlantic liners, where the officers seldom speak to the passengers except in connection with their duty.

Saturday passed pleasantly. The weather was cooler, and the Bay of Bengal, into which we had entered, was quiet and without any ground swell. It reminded me of Long Island Sound on a warm

day in August, except for the vast number of flying fishes that were to be seen.

In the evening there was an entertainment of recitations and music on the deck. Sunday, December 20th, was much like the previous day. Morning prayers were read on deck at 10.30 A. M., the captain, as usual, officiating. Just previous to the hour of service an inspection of the ship's company took place. All turned out in full uniform and formed in line; first the officers in full dress, with frock coats, then the English sailors in "apple-pie" order, with clean white trousers; and then the Lascars, also neat in white muslin clothes, with bright, new, coloured sashes around their waists, and in red turbans. In the evening the phosphorescence in the water was the most brilliant I have ever seen. One would almost imagine that there were innumerable gas-jets in the water that was disturbed by the movement of the ship.

On Monday, at one o'clock, we sighted the island of Ceylon, and ran along the shore so close that we could easily distinguish the light-houses and the trees. We passed the Point de Galle, and arrived at Colombo soon after midnight.

During our voyage several desperate heart-affairs were in progress, mostly among the officers, and on this day a prospective engagement was announced. On the Verona, from Yokohama, was a widow with several daughters, of whom one, a lovely girl, of about eighteen years, seemed rapidly to have captivated the ship's surgeon, but we thought nothing of it until we found, at Hong-Kong, that the young sawbones had been transferred to the Rosetta, so as to continue voyaging in company with his lady-love. The two were inseparable after this; and naturally the important question was asked by this young disciple of Æsculapius and a favourable reply was given, subject to mamma's approval. The widow, being the cousin of a former peer of the realm, who had been raised to his high rank for his great historical work on England, naturally considered a poor doctor to be hardly a fit match for her beautiful and blue-blooded daughter, and, though she at last yielded consent, she did not accord it quite to the young people's wishes. She insisted upon a year's probation, in hopes of curing her daughter of her fancy.

On awaking Tuesday morning, at 6 A. M., I found we were riding at anchor behind the breakwater in the harbour of Colombo. The first stone of this magnificent structure, which it took ten years to

Natives' hut in a cinnamon garden, Colombo.

complete, was laid by the Prince of Wales, December 8, 1875. Until this work was consummated Galle was the chief port of the island. The total cost of the breakwater was £700,000.

After breakfast, which was served at seven o'clock instead of nine,

A street in Colombo

I took a launch and went ashore, passed my luggage through the custom-house, and then secured a room at the Grand Oriental Hotel. The hotel was a wonderful sight, as there were six large steamships in the harbour, and their passengers were nearly all at this vast resort. With a guide I drove about, viewing the public buildings and the beautiful private bungalows, and visiting the shops. In the afternoon I inspected the Museum in the Cinnamon Gardens, and then paid a visit to Arabi Pacha. "How have the mighty fallen!" To think that the great power behind the throne who was once omnipotent in Egypt and the Soudan, and whose name and deeds engrossed the attention of all the world, should be living quietly in a very unpretending house in the suburbs of Colombo, sweltering in the hot, damp atmosphere, with no occupation and no interests in life except his negro concubines and their children!

I sent in my card, and was politely invited to enter. I found Arabi sitting on the veranda, and as I approached he rose and greeted me with much cordiality, and said with earnestness that he was pleased to see me. He then motioned me to a seat, and I sat for half an hour in conversation with him. He complained bitterly of the terrible climate of Ceylon, which he says is making him blind, besides giving him rheumatism. On my rising to leave, he again expressed his gratification at having seen me. At the gate was a nurse with Arabi's little son Abdullah, who showed unmistakable signs of his negro blood. The name of Arabi Pacha's residence is "El Sternwick."  I returned by way of the Esplanade, which is a beautiful driveway and promenade, extending along the sea from the Galle Face Hôtel to the barracks, about three fourths of a mile. It is a lovely walk, and in Ceylon, upon a fine night, certainly "every prospect pleases, and only man is vile." The band of the Gordon Highlanders was playing at the barracks, and I stopped there until the programme was rounded with the usual finale of "God save the Queen." I then took my way to the hotel in time for dinner. The

Cinnamon, Ceylon

principal buildings of Colombo are the Queen's House, the Cathedral, the Clock Tower, and the barracks.

A great many of the native Cingalese are Christians, mainly Roman Catholics. A part of the inhabitants are descendants of the first European conquerors, the Portuguese, and of the Dutch who succeeded them. The various kinds of half-castes are called Eurasians. My

Cabbage palms, Ceylon.

guide was named McDonald. He informed me that his grandfather was a soldier who had married a Cingalese woman and settled in Colombo. I tried the betel-nut, but it did not suit my palate in the least.

Colombo was named after the great Christopher Columbus, and I hoped that the people and government would be properly represented at the celebration at Chicago in 1893. The population is about 128,000; the principal business now is the shipment of tea, which has superseded that of coffee. Precious stones are found in large numbers in Ceylon. Those offered for sale are usually either of a very inferior quality or imitations, but I am inclined to think that there are few of these latter. The cutting of the stones is poor, as is also the setting, and altogether I should think that to one wishing handsome jewels they would not be satisfactory. Stones of the first quality are promptly sent to Paris and London, and are not to be found in Colombo at all.

Adam's Peak, the famous mountain of Ceylon, is considered sacred by both Mohammedans and Buddhists, in much the same way as Fusiyama in Japan. There is a depression on its summit which resembles an enormous footprint. The Mohammedans think this was where Adam stepped when he was expelled from paradise; while the Buddhists say it is the impression of Buddha's foot when he stepped from this mountain-top to Siam.

At the bungalow of the agent of the Peninsular and Oriental steamers I saw a huge tortoise, said to be over three hundred years old. The poor creature is blind, but is well taken care of.

Wednesday morning I took the train at 7.30 for Nanu-oya, and thence went by coach five miles to Nu-wara-Eliya. On leaving Colombo we passed at first for some distance through a tropical jungle, in which bamboo, and the banana, cocoa, and other palms, grew in great abundance. In the streams the natives were taking their morning bath—the men by themselves and the women and children by themselves, according to custom. The Cingalese women wear a profusion of jewellery, and their costume usually consists of a skirt of some bright colour and a white cotton waist, which modestly

Indian Bull, Colombo.

covers the bust, but is cut short so that it discloses the dark skin of the stomach and about the navel. The Tamil woman wears a skirt also, and a loose piece of red muslin neatly adjusted on one shoulder and falling gracefully over the breasts, leaving the back bare.

The Ceylon government railway is remarkably well constructed, the roadbed, bridges, and rails being substantial, and the whole work a fine piece of engineering. The cars, however, are poor, and the management is exceedingly bad. A refreshment car is run for breakfast and tiffin, and the food is fairly good.

Mustering of coolies on a tea estate, Ceylon.

At about three hours' distance from Colombo the traveller finds a change in the aspect of the country, the only crop raised being tea, with the exception of a very little coffee. The raising of tea is a comparatively new industry in Ceylon, for formerly coffee was almost the exclusive product; but the crop began to fail, and now tea has supplanted it. The dealers are making a strong effort to drive out Chinese tea in England, claiming that that of Ceylon is more wholesome. The tea estates are usually large, and many young men are

coming out from England to learn the methods of planting, as they came to the cattle-ranches in the United States a few years ago.

On arriving at Nanu-oya I found several coaches, with three large "walers," as the horses brought from New South Wales are called, driven as a "spiked team," with a coolie running alongside the leader to whip him up. The drive to Nu-wara-Eliya was superb. It was over a splendid road, for all the roads in Ceylon are excellent. In about forty minutes we arrived at the Grand Hotel, which I found to be a large bungalow, charmingly situated, and with every possible comfort. The weather was a great contrast to that of Colombo. A thick overcoat was necessary, and I was glad to warm myself before a large wood-fire. This temperature results from the altitude, the place being six thousand two hundred feet above sea level. It is the fashion among the people of elegance to go either there or to Kandy for Christmas, and many spend a month to recuperate from the incessant heat of Colombo.

Near Nu-wara-Eliya is the country of the elephants. Besides the domesticated ones, those in the wild state abound. Here also are elk, bear, red deer, leopards, moose deer, wild boar, and jungle fowl. This region is rich, too, in sapphires, rubies, and cat's-eyes, and in gold and tin.

Dinner, at 7.30, was much like that meal in private houses, the table being tastefully decorated with flowers. The vegetables served included cabbage, turnips, and celery, all raised in the neighbourhood —which was strange, considering how near we were to the equator. That night, being furnished with a good bed, I slept better than at any time since leaving Hong-Kong.

On Thursday morning I had "*chota hazri*," or early tea, with toast, butter, and jam, brought to me by a boy, according to the invariable custom in Ceylon and India, after which I went for a long drive, returning by coach in time for breakfast at ten o'clock.

At 12.30 the coach stopped for me, and I drove back to Nanu-oya, whence I took the train for Kandy, having received a telegram that my room there was ready for me.

The principal crops grown in this part of Ceylon, besides tea and coffee, are cocoa, cinchona, cardamoms, cotton, tobacco, India-rubber, pepper, cloves, mace, rice, sugar, and nutmegs.

Double bullock-carts, Colombo.

The large traffic of Christmas-time delayed my train, which was over an hour late when it reached Kandy. On Christmas day, at seven o'clock, the boy awoke me and conducted me down to the

Buddhist Temple at Kandy.

bath, which was among the horse-stalls adjoining the street. The bath-tub was of primitive order, being made of cement, and looking much like a fish-pond, but it answered the purpose as well as the fine porcelain ones that are found in American hotels. After tea I took a guide and a carriage and went for a beautiful drive around the lake or the tank, as it is called, passing through Lady MacCarthy's Road and Lady Gordon's Road to Lady Horton's Walk. These mountains entirely shut in the ancient capital. The view of the range surrounding Kandy is very fine. My guide pointed out to me specimens of nutmeg, cinnamon, rattan, breadfruit, pepper, and cloves. We then descended the hill, passing the English church of St. Paul's, where an early Christmas service was being held, and thence to the former pal-

ace of the kings, which includes the Dalada Maliga Wa, or temple of the sacred tooth of Buddha. Here also service was being held by Buddhist priests, and strains of the Christian organ blended with the pounding of the heathen tom-tom. There I saw the gilded receptacle which is said to contain the tooth. The original tooth, though, was undoubtedly destroyed by the Portuguese conquerors in 1560. In the Museum at Colombo I saw a facsimile of the object which is now averred to be the tooth. It resembles more the tusk of a wild boar then any mandible of the human mouth. The receptacles for the teeth of Buddha number seven, and are studded with precious stones of fabulous value. There are other interesting sights in the temple, notably an image of Buddha cut in crystal. Opposite to the Temple of the Sacred Tooth is a Hindoo temple sacred to Vishnu, in the compound or yard of which is a sacred bo tree, and a copy in stone of the footprint of Adam which he impressed on Adam's Peak when he alighted from his fall out of paradise.

At 11 A. M. I attended St. Paul's Church. Here I witnessed a full cathedral service excellently rendered, and it was gratifying to see many Cingalese among the congregation. How different must have been the scene of kindred devotions at Grace Church, New

Entrance to gardens at Peredeniya, near Colombo.

York, where I had attended services on so many previous Christmas days! There had been no attempts here at dressing the church with greens, but there was a beautiful floral display. As to the service,

Sorting tea leaves, Ceylon

the splendid old ritual of the Anglican Church sounds grand and impressive the world over.

After luncheon I visited the botanical gardens at Përadeniya, four miles distant. I was delighted at the fine collection of tropical trees, and of orchids and other plants, concerning whose names and nature an attendant gave me what information I sought. I was especially interested in the giant bamboos, and the mahogany, banyan, and deadly upas trees. I then took the train for Colombo, arriving in time for an excellent Christmas dinner, with a *menu* comprising roast turkey, which I washed down with some dry champagne.

Saturday morning I took a catamaran and went out to look at the accommodations on board the British India steamer Anna, which plies between Colombo and Tuticorin. I found her to be very small, and with only one cabin of two berths for first-class passengers, the

Castor-oil making, Penang.

steamer having been intended for the transportation of coolies only. However, I secured the cabin for the following noon.

The island of Ceylon is a crown colony, and is in no way connected with her Majesty's Indian Empire. In 1888 the population of the whole island was estimated at 2,800,000, and that of the city of Colombo at 120,000. The export of tea increased from twenty-three pounds in 1876 to 24,000,000 pounds in 1888, while there has been a similar increase in that of cinchona-bark, from an output of 12,000 pounds in 1872 to one of 15,000,000 pounds in 1888. Large quantities of plumbago, the finest in the world, are mined in the interior of Ceylon by the natives.

The future of this island colony I should suppose to be bright. With good government, economically administered, among industrious and peaceable inhabitants, the increase of wealth must be very rapid.

The Sacred Bull of Siva.

CHAPTER VII.

IN HINDOSTAN.

ON Sunday, December 27, 1891, at 11.30 A. M., I took a boat and went on board the British India steamer Amra, Captain Costello, a vessel of four hundred tons burden. The ship was surrounded by bumboats and catamarans conveying to her decks loads of coolies, about three hundred and fifty in all, who were making their way back to various parts of the Madras Presidency. At 12.30 we sailed out of the Colombo roadstead, passing the Messagerie Maritime steamer, which was just arriving from Hong-Kong and Singapore. Our captain soon made his appearance, and I found him an agreeable and bright young Irishman, who had been educated in France. I inquired of him about the sea-snakes in these waters; and he said he had frequently seen them, and that if a rope was thrown overboard when a ship was lying still in a calm they would crawl up to the vessel's deck.

In company with the dirty, half-clad natives on the Amra was an English member of the Salvation Army. This organization is making a strong effort to Christianize the people of Ceylon, and, in order to reach them the more effectually, it has adopted for its agents an adaptation of the native dress, consisting of a red turban and shirt and yellow skirt falling to the feet, which are bare both of stockings and of shoes. Women dress as the men do, with the exception that they have nothing on their heads, but they carry an umbrella to protect themselves from the fierce rays of the sun. The excitement among the coolies in Colombo was intense at the time I was there; for General Booth, the head of the army, had just departed thence, after holding meetings to stir religionists to greater activity. The "soldiers" who have come over from England to devote themselves to religious duty are undoubtedly disinterested enthusiasts, for their lives cannot be pleasant; but I should think their zeal was sometimes misdirected. Their efforts should be to elevate the people they come to convert. Associating with the natives as they do, they lower themselves and injure the prestige of all Europeans. Still, one should not judge them harshly, for their aim assuredly is to do a good work for Christianity.

We soon got out of sight of land, and were on our way across the Gulf of Manar, which is very apt to be roughened by the monsoon. The skipper, as the captain was called, informed me that these waters are somewhat like the English Channel. At the head of this gulf there is a series of islands and rocks, named Adam's Bridge, which extends to the coast of India. The channel at Paumben Passage is but an eighth of a mile wide.

Toward night the wind increased until a heavy sea was running, and soon this was reënforced by a hard rain, and I was obliged to take refuge in my cabin. Thinking that the best thing to do would be to go to sleep, I undressed, and attempted it; but the air was so warm and close that sleep was impossible. The cabin was in the extreme stern of the ship, and the motion was particularly disagreeable. In addition to these discomforts, a vast number of cockroaches were running about in all directions, and, although harmless, they were decidedly unpleasant.

At eight o'clock we cast anchor five miles from Tuticorin, and, as the sea was so rough, the steam-launch did not dare to come out to us, but instead three large lighters made their appearance. The coolies filled these, and it was with considerable difficulty that I managed to get upon one of them. The trip from the steamer to the shore was wet and uncomfortable, and the crowd of coolies, some of whom had leprosy, were not greatly desirable company. At last we landed, and after passing the customs I proceeded to the hotel, each of my five pieces of luggage being carried on the head of a single coolie. The usual dispute occurred over their pay, but I had become wonted to this noisy altercation, and, after giving all concerned a liberal recompense, I left them to go away at their

Mother of woman, is it difficult to Indian woman of lower caste.

leisure, without more concern on my part, since they would never be satisfied, no matter how large a sum they received. I was so much exhausted that it was difficult to eat, but after luncheon I felt better. This was the most fatiguing and unpleasant voyage that I have yet taken, but happily it was short.

At 2.15 I left Tuticorin, which is a place of no special interest, except perhaps in the fact that the inhabitants are nearly all Roman

Catholics, having been converted many years ago by the Portuguese. The South Indian Railway is of narrow gauge, only three feet three and five eighths inches wide, but well constructed and managed for a road over which nearly all who travel are natives. The carriages have a little awning of tin or wood, and the roadbed is fenced for its whole distance with a hedge of cactus.

I noticed here for the first time that certain of the natives wear stripes of red, and that others of different caste, who worship different gods, wear white stripes; sometimes a round dot on the forehead is the sign. The Indian women of all castes carry their children on their left hip, with the child's face toward the bearer's body. These women wear immense quantities of jewellery, both of gold and silver, made into innumerable ear-rings, nose-rings, and toe-rings, and bangles that encincture their upper arms, wrists, and ankles.

The railway time-table is kept on the twenty-four-hour system, the same that the Western line of the Canadian Pacific Railway has adopted, and it is said to simplify matters very much.

The country through which I passed was flat and uninteresting. Great numbers of cattle, buffalo, sheep, and goats were grazing in the fields, and considerable quantities of rice and cotton are raised in the neighbourhood. The climate proved a most agreeable change from that of Ceylon.

On arriving at Madura, at 8 P. M., I found that the two rooms in the station for the use of travellers were taken, so that I was obliged to sleep in the waiting-room on a cane-bottomed lounge.

On December 29th, in the morning, after early tea, I engaged a guide and drove to the Great Temple. This is considered the finest in southern India. It is a remarkable building, with its wonderful specimens of Hindu carving, its thousand-pillared hall, and its curious tank, where in the dirty-green water the devotees cleanse themselves thoroughly, as they suppose, before worshipping. Thence we drove out to see an enormous banyan tree, which has over a hundred large roots growing from branches that have bent to the ground. I went

The Hall of Horses, Seringham.

next to the Teppa Kulam, or great tank, about a mile and a half outside the city. In the centre of the tank is a square island on which stands a beautiful temple. Once a year, when the idol from the Great Temple is brought here, the little island glitters with ten thousand lights. The palace of Tirumala is a splendid specimen of architecture. It is to some extent a restoration, made at considerable expense by the English, and is used for government purposes.

Brass work, silver work, and gold work, and the manufacture of cloths stained in a peculiar manner, are the specialties of Madura. Many of the natives are Christians, mostly Roman Catholics; but American missionaries are at work in this district, and the inhabitants who have relations with their missions number about seven thousand.

After breakfast I boarded the train for Trichinopoly, taking with me Jacob, my guide, who is a Wesleyan Methodist. The natives in addressing Europeans always call them " Master " or " Your Honour," and the policemen give the military salute to foreigners. At 6 P. M. we arrived at Trichinopoly, where a room awaited me, for which I had applied by telegram. In India there are three classes of telegrams—urgent, ordinary, and deferred—with corresponding grades of cost. At the refreshment rooms there are usually two bed-rooms, and the sojourner can spend the night comfortably, but the next day he must move on; it is not permitted to him to remain longer.

On December 30th I took a carriage early in the morning, and with my guide Jacob drove first to the temples at Seringham, which is an island lying between the Cauvery and Coloroon. These temples cover a large area, and I spent considerable time in investigating them, having all the beautiful jewels that are used to decorate the gods brought out and shown to me by the custodian. The Hall of Horses contains fine specimens of carving. In the streets of the temples sacred cows wander around, and elephants are led by their keepers.

I climbed up Trichinopoly Rock, which is like a huge boulder rising directly out of the plain, two hundred and seventy-three feet above the land at its base. This fortress is conspicuous from all sides, and is a most picturesque object. It is ascended by a series of steps in a covered passage, with a shorter flight of steps to the Siva temple at the extreme apex.

Trichinopoly has been the scene of several celebrated sieges, and it played an important part in the Karnatic struggles. In 1881 the

Trichinopoly Rock and Tank.

population was eighty-four thousand souls, about eleven thousand of whom were Christians. In the principal tank there, on April 3, 1826, Bishop Reginald Heber, author of the grand old missionary hymn, "From Greenland's icy mountains," was drowned while bathing. At the temple I saw many Brahmans, both men and women. They can be distinguished readily from the other castes, not only by their dress but by their different aspect as a race. At first the caste feeling in India strikes an alien as very strange. While coming down the long flight of steps at Trichinopoly Rock we met a number of Brahman women, very poor, and with hardly any clothing, carrying up brass kettles containing water, which they first take to the temple to have it blessed before they use it in their households. While carrying this water they must not touch or even approach any one of another caste; and as we approached these poor women they called out, asking us not to come too near them. It seemed ridiculous that these wretched creatures should be afraid of contamination from clean and respectable foreigners.

Going back to the station I proceeded by train to Tanjore, an hour's journey. Tanjore is full of historical interest, and its great temple has a world-wide reputation. On my arrival I secured a cart drawn by a fleet pair of young bullocks, and drove first to the temple. Here I was surprised to find how superb was the great pagoda. In size and in the beauty of its carving it is without doubt the finest of its style in India. Halfway between the temple entrance and the pagoda is the celebrated Nandi, or sacred bull of Siva. It is in a crouching posture under a stone canopy. The bull is sixteen feet in length, seven feet in width, and twelve feet two inches in height, measured to the top of the head. It is cut from one solid block of syenite, and the anointing of it with oil and the subsequent polishing it gets daily have given it the appearance of bronze.

The town is entirely surrounded by a fort and a moat constructed by the former kings. The citadel contains a small Christian church built by the famous missionary of early times, Schwartz, whose handsome white marble memorial was shown to me by an attendant.

I then visited the palace of the former rajahs. It is of great extent, and in the Nayakar Durbar Hall is a fine statue in marble of the Rajah Sivaji. This is placed upon the huge flat stone on which the Mahratta kings sat when administering justice. On the ramparts is the great gun made of rings of iron and brass. This gun measures twenty-four feet five inches in length, and it has a bore of two feet two inches. It has been fired only once. It survived the experiment, but would hardly stand another trial. Tanjore is well worth a visit, and it is surprising that the railway company does not provide rooms in the station for the use of travellers. There is, however, a dak bungalow where one can be comfortable.

At 8.15 I took the train for Madras. Among the hills of the Madras Presidency live the Todas. They are tall, well-proportioned, and athletic, and have a bold, independent manner. Their means of livelihood is tending their herds of cattle. The chief interest attaching to them is the fact that they practise polyandry, all the brothers of a family marrying one woman; and, strange to say, the children of these marriages are exceptionally fine in health and appearance. It is amusing, by the way, to see the little brown-skinned babies in India without a stitch of clothing. As they grow older they are particular to cover themselves—not with a fig-leaf, but with a piece of cloth about the same size.

The night journey from Tanjore occupied just twelve hours. I arrived at Madras at 8.15 A. M. The Indian railway carriages are constructed so as to enable each first-class passenger to recline at full length during night journeys, and are also fitted with lavatories. Passengers must provide themselves with soap, towels, pillows, and rugs. My first experience was not pleasant, as the carriage rattled and shook too much to allow the possibility of sleep.

On arriving at the station in Madras, December 31st, I was beset by an army of coolies, each wanting to carry my luggage. The result

Jain idols conveyed in bullock cart.

was that I paid five for carrying the things (about one hundred and seventy-five pounds weight), one for showing the way to a *gharry*, and, of course, the coachman and footman—making eight in all. Several others demanded money for some imaginary service, but these I refused. How different are the people here from those of Japan, where everything is made pleasant for travellers, and no annoyances are experienced! I remained at the Elphinstone Hotel until the afternoon, when I took a *gharry* and went for a drive through the town.

Madras is not a compactly built city; it spreads over a large area. The Government buildings are fine, but the general appearance is not one of prosperity. Fort St. George contains a number of public offices within its walls, it being the site of the original "factory" or settlement made in 1639 by Francis Day. Madras was the earliest British acquisition in India, and was itself known at first as Fort St. George, which name subsequently gave place to the present one.

The most remarkable object in Madras is the artificial harbour, which was opened for shipping in 1881. It is built of huge concrete blocks, and shaped into two arms extending at right angles from the beach, for there was no natural harbour whatever. This cost a large sum of money, but it has been of immense advantage, as it not only provides safe moorings for the vessels of all nations, but has made possible the construction of an iron pier for landing passengers and goods. Formerly this landing was effected in *masullah* boats, through the surf.

I had received the proffer of the hospitalities of the Madras Club, which occupies a handsome house with a large number of bedrooms, but I preferred the independence of hotel life. At sunset I went to hear the band play on the Marine Promenade, which runs directly along the Bay of Bengal, separated therefrom by a sand beach only. It is delightful there in the evening, and the promenade is frequented by the European residents and the rich natives. It was an interesting scene, this mixture of the descendants of the English conquerors and of those who had been subjugated. The Indian gentlemen were richly dressed, and each was accompanied by several servants.

My room at the Elphinstone Hotel was on the ground floor, and soon after my arrival I was visited by several snake-charmers, jugglers, and sword-swallowers. Some of these are very expert in their tricks, one of which—to make the mango tree grow from a seed—is wonderfully well done.

I had been obliged to engage a "boy," as a servant is called, at the hotel immediately on my arrival, this procedure being expected here. The guests are supposed, too, to bring their own pillows and blankets or rugs. The charge for working the *punkah* (a large fan) all night is about two annas, equal to four cents. I slept well that night, after the shaking up in the train I had the night before.

On New-Year's day, 1892, I was awakened early by a salute fired in honour of the New Year, and soon afterward my boy brought me *chota hazri* and prepared my bath. A great many natives were congregated about the hotel, and I learned that they had come with little gifts to their patrons, of course expecting a substantial New-Year's present in return. Every place being closed on account of the holidays, I spent the morning quietly in reading up India. The principal street in Madras is Mount Road, and here are the best retail shops, in large, detached houses, in the centre of a compound or garden. I never have seen this arrangement elsewhere. St. George's Anglican Cathedral, the old Botanical Gardens, the Madras Club, and the various hotels are also on this road.

The People's Park and Robinson's Park are delightful resorts for the public's relaxation and pleasure; and surrounding Government House, which is a stately building, there is a fine palm garden.

A pretty drive from the city takes one to Little Mount and the spot where St. Thomas the apostle is said to have been martyred (A. D. 68) by infuriated Brahmans, who, after pelting him with stones, transfixed him on a spear. On the summit of the mount is a chapel over a cave, wherein the saint is said to have lived. His body is

A snake-charmer.

buried, tradition avers, under the Portuguese cathedral of St. Thomé, erected in 1606.

Madras has probably more Christians in proportion to its population than any other Indian city. Out of 432,000 persons, about 50,000 belong to the various denominations.

At 5 P. M. I drove through the beautiful grounds of Government House to Fort St. George, which is always garrisoned by English regiments, for even now the native troops are not entirely trusted. I was much interested to see, in St. Mary's Church, a very old building within the fort, the memorial of Major-General Sir John Burgoyne, and outside, facing the barracks, the marble statue of Lord Cornwallis, surrounded by captured bronze cannon. The former well-known name suggests that of the other General John Burgoyne. Both these names are familiar in the United States, linked with great disasters to Britain's prestige and to her hopes of control in the New World—the surrenders at Saratoga and at Yorktown—whereby the independence of the British colonies was assured, and the birth of a new nation, destined to be greater and richer than its progenitor, became an accomplished fact.

From the fort I drove along the Marine Promenade, the day (a *fête*-day) being particularly gay and interesting. This drive, with its walk, extends over two miles along the sea, somewhat like the Promenade des Anglais at Nice, and is a most pleasant part of Madras. I remained enjoying the cool breezes until it became quite dark, and the young moon and the stars twinkling in the heavens were to be seen, when I returned to the hotel just in time for an eight-o'clock dinner.

On Sunday, January 3d, in the morning I attended service at St. George's Cathedral. This is a capacious building of Grecian architecture. The interior is white. On the walls are many memorial tablets of English officials. *Punkahs*, worked without, were kept in motion during service. The boy choir, principally composed of Eurasians, executed the music remarkably well; but Asiatics have not the sweet voices and taste for music that the negroes have. Toward sunset I went for a walk along the beach, and spent some time in watching the natives fishing in the surf on their rafts, which are made of four logs lashed together.

The depreciation of silver is a great injury to India, China, and, in fact, all Asiatic countries, where it is the sole currency. It seems odd that England does not join with the United States in adopting a bimetallic currency. All Europeans complain that the payment in gold for everything they buy at home adds largely to the price. There is no doubt that the remonetization of silver would add greatly to the prosperity and wealth of England's Indian empire.

On Monday, January 4th, at eleven o'clock, I took a *masullah* boat with ten rowers, and, after some difficulty in getting through the surf, finally reached the Messagerie Maritime steamer Nieman, of about eighteen hundred tons, Captain Louis Flager. We left the harbour of Madras at 2 P.M. on our way for Calcutta. On board I found, to my pleasure and surprise, a half-dozen passengers whom I had met on the Rosetta. There was also on board Monsieur Clement-Thomas, the French Governor of Pondicherry, going for a visit to Calcutta. On Tuesday the weather was delightful, compared with that of Ceylon and southern India. I had a long talk with two Brahman gentlemen in the Government service, who explained the caste system of India most clearly. They were young men of fine attainments, and they understood thoroughly the history and politics of both Europe and the United States.

CHAPTER VIII.

UP THE GANGES.

IN the early morning of Thursday, January 7th, we anchored at the mouth of the Hooghly River, about eighty miles from Calcutta, off a low, sandy shore resembling Fire Island, near New York. We were obliged to wait until the tide served, at about 12.30 P. M., whereupon we continued up the river to Diamond Bay and anchored for the night. The Ganges and the Brahmaputra unite their waters and flow into the Bay of Bengal by several mouths, the principal one being the Hooghly; and in the morning I took my bath in Ganges water, which the Hindus regard as sacred. The shores, as we proceeded up to Diamond Harbour, were low, in some places the land being protected from inundation by an embankment, or, as it would be called on the Mississippi, a levee.

The steamer Niemen I found a well-managed and comfortable ship, although it was small, and I believe the universal testimony is favourable to the Messageries Maritime lines. The service is excellent and the food good.

On Friday morning at daybreak we attempted to resume our voyage, but, to our disgust, we found that the ship was grounded. With much difficulty she got into the channel and went on. On the banks of the Hooghly are many jute plantations, and near the city are factories for the preparation of the raw material. At eleven o'clock the Niemen was attached to her buoys at Calcutta. As Madras was the place at which I had embarked on the ship, I was not subjected to any customs examination, and as soon as possible I secured a *budgerow*, was towed to the ghat, or landing-place, and went immediately to the Great Eastern Hotel.

Calcutta has been described as a city of palaces, and the various public buildings, such as the Government House, the residence of the viceroy, the Belvidere, the residence of the Lieutenant Governor of Bengal, the High Court, the Imperial Museum, and St. Paul's Cathedral, are imposing edifices. The streets are well paved and clean. The principal ones are those in the neighbourhood of the Maidan, the Chowringhee Road, and Old Courthouse Street. In the Zoölogical Garden are some fine specimens of Bengal tigers, besides other animals indigenous to India. Calcutta, when it was settled in 1690, was called by the English Fort William. The site of the famous Black Hole and the old fort can now hardly be traced, for the present city is entirely modern.

As soon as possible I secured the services, as valet or boy, of a Portuguese Eurasian named Pedro, and after tiffin took a victoria and visited the Zoölogical Gardens, and the famous Temple of Kali, from whom the city of Calcutta derives its name. This Hindu goddess is the patron of the Thugs, and is known as The Black or Bloody One. She is represented as dripping with blood, with a necklace of infants' skulls, is the deity of famine and pestilence, and is said to be appeasable only by bloody sacrifices.

There were many worshippers when we arrived at the temple, but

Drawing toddy in Bengal.

a rupee given to one of the priests was the cause of a general exodus on the part of the assemblage, so that I was able to see the idol—from the outside, for the temple is considered too sacred for a foreigner to enter. The surroundings were dirty, and in my disgust at these I could not help thinking what a curse religious creeds have been to all countries from the earliest times. A trip to a heathen country would be a good education for many a narrow-minded clergyman of Europe or America.

On our return we followed the beautiful drive along the river, passing Fort William. Here we saw all the beauty and fashion of India's capital, both European and native. They were taking the afternoon drive, or riding, or engaged with cricket or golf in the Maidan. At the Eden Garden a military band was playing, and many of the carriage occupants alighted for a half hour to listen to the music.

There is a curious industry in the streets of Calcutta: men carry water-pipes for the accommodation of passers-by, and the wayfarer, upon payment of a small sum, may stop for a moment and take a few whiffs of tobacco.

At dinner, on the first night of my arrival, I discovered that in India *champagne frappé* is usually known as "Simpkins"—for what reason I am unable to say.

On Saturday morning we drove to the Botanical Gardens, which are at a considerable distance from the city. These are well worth a visit, being a most attractive pleasure-ground. The great banyan tree is the largest I have seen; it has two hundred and thirty-two air roots, and its diameter, inclusive of the roots, is three hundred feet. The original trunk is about a hundred years old and is still standing. Returning from the Botanical Gardens, I looked through the admirable collection of the Imperial Museum, and, having purchased bedding and pillows—which it is necessary to carry in India—at four o'clock I left Calcutta from Sealdah Station by the mail train on the Eastern Bengal State Railway. This road is of standard gauge, well built, ballasted with stone, and laid with iron ties, while the telegraph poles are of sheet iron rolled up and riveted together. At Damookdea Ghât the passengers were transferred to a large stern-wheel steamboat, which carried them over the Ganges, nearly three miles across. Dinner was served on board. We landed at Para Ghât, the beginning of the Northern Bengal State Railway, the gauge of which is known as metre-gauge, being three feet, three and five-eighths inches wide. I secured a compartment, had Pedro make up the bed, and rested fairly well until we reached Siliguri, at 7 A. M. on Sunday, January 10th. Here came a change to the Darjeeling Himalayan Railway—a remarkable engineering work, comparable with the St. Gothard or the Denver and Rio Grande Railway. Its gauge is only two feet, the same as that of the little road in the Jardin des Plantes in Paris, and it follows the splendid cart-road, though with frequent deviations. The speed of the train is but seven miles an hour, the ascent per hour being one thousand feet. The little carriages, some open and others closed, and the tiny engine, looked like those of a toy train. The ascent begins after seven miles of travel through the Terai plains, and from that point it is one of the most beautiful rides that I can remember, similar to the trip from Vera Cruz to the City of Mexico. Lofty mountains tower above, while dense forest and jungles spread away to the right and left. At two o'clock we stopped at Kurseong for luncheon, and the keen cold air (for by this time I was wearing my heaviest winter overcoat and was wrapped in a heavy rug) had given me a sharp appetite. This point is 4,860 feet above sea level, and twenty miles from Darjeeling. In two hours more we arrived there, and we walked up the steep hill to the Woodlands Hotel. I had telegraphed for a room, and it was now ready, with a soft-coal fire burning in it. This I found very comfortable, as the altitude is 7,200 feet and the weather was frosty. Darjeeling is the sanitarium not only of Calcutta but of the whole of Bengal, and scattered about it are many beautiful villas, mostly built of stone in European fashion. The temperature never rises above

Nepaulese Ranee and attendants.

DARJEELING. IN THE HILLS.

78° nor falls below 30°. The pleasure during the summer season of the change from the terrible heat of the plains to this bracing air may be imagined.

In conversation with me, an Anglo-Indian drew a most unpleasant picture of the state of European society throughout India. The wives and children of English officials are sent every summer to Simla, Darjeeling, and other cool spots in the hills; and freedom from home restraint soon has its effect on the ladies, especially the young wives, who go step by step from innocent flirtation until they forget their marriage vows. The manners prevailing at these resorts are informal, and the effect, it is said, is very demoralizing. I have heard similar stories; but no doubt they are much exaggerated, for immorality is exceptional among Anglo-Saxon women in every clime.

The Maharajah of Burmah.

Sunday being the market day, as soon as I got my room arranged I went down to the bazaar, which is one of the sights of India. It was thronged with hill people—Lepchas, Thibetans, Nepaulese, and other races and tribes—the Mongolian cast of countenance predominating. Buddhist lamas also are frequently seen in the crowd. These hill people are polyandrous, and in many instances one woman lives in the hut with five men. The women are large, and have smiling faces; they usually wear several rows of turquoise and coarse beads around their necks, enormous rings of the same style in their ears, and on their fingers a dozen silver rings.

Monday morning, before daybreak, Pedro called me and brought in tea, and after dressing hurriedly I set out for Tiger Hill, six miles distant. It was six o'clock, and still quite dark. In about an hour and a quarter we reached our destination. The road all the way had been extremely picturesque; and my first view of Kinchinjunga was the sublimest scene I have ever witnessed. The Matterhorn, the Jungfrau, Mont Blanc, and Mount Pilatus were as nothing compared with Gaurisanker (Mount Everest) and Kinchinjunga. The view extends beyond the boundaries of the Indian Empire, for some of the mountains seen are in Thibet.

The spectator, standing at his finest view-point, looks north and northwest. On the right, due north, is Kinchinjunga, 28,165 feet high, and forty-five miles away. On the left, northwest, is Mount Everest, 29,002 feet high, and a hundred and seven miles distant. Between these two highest mountains in the world the sky is serrated by a lofty white line of perpetual snow. The middle distance is filled with mountain ranges, mostly snowy, which are only less gigantic than their great neighbours; and in the foreground of the picture we look upon heavily wooded hills, with rivers winding among them and occasionally plunging through deep gorges. The lamas have their monasteries on many of the peaks. The Jelepla Pass, through which trade is carried on with Thibet, is open all the year round.

In the afternoon I took a "dandy," which is a variety of palanquin, with four coolies as carriers, and went to the Bhutea Bustee, or village, two miles from the Woodlands Hotel. I stopped at the Buddhist temple, where the attendant lamas showed me prayer wheels in motion. Buddhism originated in India at Benares, but it is now practically extinct there; and the few temples along the northern frontier are quite different in the beliefs and practices in vogue at their altars from those of Japan, China, and Siam, while those in Ceylon differ from all the others. On Tuesday morning we had another splendid view of Kinchinjunga from the hotel, and at 11 A. M. we took our leave of Darjeeling, retracing our route, and arriving at Calcutta at 11.20 P. M.

Wednesday, January 13th, I rested quietly at the Great Eastern

The highest mountain in the world, viewed from Darjeeling.

Hotel until late in the afternoon, when I took a delightful drive in the Maidan, meeting many of the English and natives of distinction, and left in the night train, at nine o'clock, for Benares. One disagreeable feature of Indian tours is the necessity of night travel; frequently there are no day trains. I took my departure from the Howrah Station, on the other side of the river, which is crossed on a handsome bridge.

On Thursday morning, at twelve, we arrived at Moghal Sarai, when we changed from the East Indian to the Oude and Rohilkund Railway, and in forty-five minutes we arrived at Benares, and were soon comfortably settled at Clark's Family Hotel. The East Indian Railway is very like a railway in England, and at the refreshment rooms excellent meals are furnished by G. F. Kellner & Co., whose establishments are managed in much the same manner as those of Spiers & Pond, who have monopolized this business on the railway systems of Great Britain. Benares is the fifth in size among Indian cities, and is noted for its ornamental brass work as well as for its embroideries and brocades. Only a few hundred Christians reside there, the rest of the population being Hindus and Mohammedans. In all probability it is the most ancient town in India, and it bears the same relation to Brahmanism that Jerusalem bears to the Christian faith and Mecca to Islamism. Benares also was the birthplace of Buddhism, and thence Buddha sent forth his missionaries to the other nations of Asia, until his system of religious belief was professed by half the population of the world. The Buddhism of Benares ceased to exist many centuries ago, but the ruins of some of its sacred buildings still remain at Sarnath, about four miles out of the town.

Benares is on the Ganges, that sacred stream which every devout Hindu wishes to visit before he dies, therein to wash away his sins. No matter what crime he has committed, a bath in these waters cleanses his soul and renders his future life happy. Some pilgrims follow the river from its source to its mouth and then back again. Ganges water is distributed throughout India as the most precious gift that a Hindu can bestow upon a cherished relative or friend.

Most of the temples and shrines in Benares are devoted to the worship of Siva and of his terrible wife, who is known under different names. The only spots sacred to Vishnu, the other principal Hindu god, are the famous Well of Mani-karnika and the stone representing his footprints. Vishnu is worshipped by the educated class of Hindus, and is supposed to possess the highest traits of character, while Siva is a terrible, cruel, and bloodthirsty deity, the god of the disgusting fakirs, who disfigure themselves, practise horrid rites, and eat carrion and excrement.

A Benares fakir, or mendicant.

After a good hot bath and an excellent luncheon at the hotel I drove, with a local native guide, about three miles to the river, took a *budgerow*, and was rowed up, stopping along the way to see the Nepaulese temple, ascending the minaret of the mosque built by the Great Mogul Aurungzebe, among the numerous Hindu fanes, and seeing various other objects of interest.

The mosque is a wonderful piece of architecture. Its foundation begins far below the bed of the river and is very massive. From this rise the walls of the square edifice in graceful outline, and crowning all are the domes and minarets. These minarets are slender stems of stone, only eight feet in diameter, and rise to the height of a hundred and fifty feet from the floor of the mosque, or about three hundred feet above the river.

Returning, we stopped for an hour and viewed the whole process of cremating the dead at the Burning Ghât. The body of a person

Method of burning the dead on the banks of the sacred Ganges.

deceased, half an hour after death, is brought from his home to the Ganges, wrapped in a cloth and secured upon two bamboo poles carried by coolies. The body is at once dipped in the river, to cleanse it from sin; it is then laid on the shore, and a pyre of wood is constructed. Then the nearest relative approaches with a barber, who shaves the face of the corpse, and after that shaves the chief mourner, who then takes a bath in the Ganges. Coming out of the water, the chief mourner, with assistance, places the body on the pyre, covering it up carefully with wood; and then, from fire kept for the purpose, fetching on a handful of straw some coals, he walks around the pyre five times. When he has done this he applies the torch to the wood until it burns briskly. At the end of two hours the bones and ashes are thrown into the river, the cinders are swept up, and the place is arranged for another cremation. The surroundings are disgusting, and dogs and crows are usually looking on, attracted by the burning flesh.

I remained until the sun went down, and the scene was weird and strange. As soon as night sets in many women come down to the ghâts, burn camphor as an offering to the Ganges, and pray for strong and healthy male offspring.

On Friday morning, January 15th, we drove early to the river and embarked in a *budgerow*, which was rowed slowly past the whole front of the city. The Ganges was filled with pilgrims washing themselves in the holy water. This was a remarkable sight. There were thousands of natives, in all conditions of life and of all ages, including the fakirs, cripples, and holy Brahman beggars. Roaming about among them were dogs, pigs, sheep, goats, and, of course, many of the sacred bulls and cows. At the Burning Ghât upright stones were pointed out to me as marking the spots where in former times widows had been burned with their husbands. This practice was stopped by the British authorities, and widows are now allowed to live in peace; but they must have their heads always closely shaved. Their appearance is very queer, especially that of the younger ones.

In this trip we occupied more than three hours, going back to the Ghat whence we started. We then took breakfast and went to the native town, visiting, besides many shops in the bazaar, the Golden Temple (the most sacred spot in Benares), the "Well of Knowledge," and the Cow Temple. All these were disappointing, being small, and dirty beyond description. After this we drove out to the Durga Temple, known to Europeans generally as the Monkey Temple. I bought some parched corn and amused myself by feeding a group of monkeys, some of which were very large. Formerly there were two thousand here, but they were such a pest to the neighbourhood that the authorities transported all but about thirty to a neighbouring jungle.

Just before leaving, I saw a goat sacrificed by a priest. This is one of the few Hindu temples where animals are thus offered up to

Bullock cart, Benares.

the gods. The priest cut off the goat's head with one stroke of a large sword. The head was placed on a block or altar, after which the carcass, except a certain part retained as toll, was returned to the person who made the offering. When pious Hindus think it is time to kill a goat, instead of doing the slaughtering themselves they have the animal decapitated at the Durga Temple, thus propitiating the god, and the flesh is restored to them to be used for food.

Returning to the river, we took a boat up the Ganges to the palace of the Maharajah of Benares, and, after sending in my card, I was courteously received and shown through the state apartments by a secretary. The palace is on the opposite side of the river from Be-

Place containing impression of Vishnu's feet in stone, at Benares.

nares, on the edge of the water, and is really a fortified castle, with a detachment of the Maharajah soldiers on guard at the gate.

This finished the sight-seeing for the day, and I am sorry to admit that I was disappointed, on the whole, in the city, the temples, and the mosques. As for Brahmanism, it is too vile for description, the emblem of Siva being a fit symbol of its disgusting character. Its principles and practices are degrading, and it would be a great boon to India if these should be modified or abolished by the British rulers, as were *suttee*, or widow immolation, and child marriages. The breaking down of caste is absolutely essential to the progress of civilization among the natives. But prejudice is still so strong, that those natives who are educated and refined are afraid to come out openly and denounce a condition of affairs that they do not hesitate to condemn in conversation with Europeans. A few Hindu maxims, translated from the Kural of Tirukuller, will indicate the low moral tone that finally results from such a religion:

> Blessed the man who never lacks
> Asafœtida, ghee, and jacks.
>
> Cursed the man, whatever his worth,
> Who is poor in purse and low in birth.
>
> The unity of the Tamilian nation
> Is cemented by caste and litigation.
>
> What "master pleases" be careful to do,
> And be cheating him while he's beating you.
>
> 'Tis good to eat; but keep your pice,
> And, if you can manage it, steal the rice.
>
> When you hear the cry "Murder!" run away;
> The police will take you up if you stay.
>
> If you beat a man, swear he beat you;
> And to his one witness bring you two.
>
> That man is a fool, whoever he be,
> Who would not do anything for a rupee.

If you don't wish them to annihilate you,
Conciliate devils—and white men too!

A botheration, a useless vexation,
To the Tamil nation is sanitation.

Municipalities always tell lies;
The census is only a tax in disguise.

Why tax us for bridges and roads? In our lives
We need but three things—gold, lands, and wives.

To cook for man, woman chiefly was meant;
Ignorance is her best ornament.

Saturday morning a juggler and snake-charmer appeared at my door and informed me that he had succeeded in catching several cobras, as I had told him to do, and that he was ready to show me how quickly his little mongoose could kill them. He had the snakes, which were large, in an earthen jar, and took out four in succession, placing them on the ground; at once the mongoose seized them, and after a short struggle dispatched the reptile, but not without getting several severe bites himself. After this the juggler gave me an exhibition of his tricks, and I found him an expert at his trade.

At 12.45 I left Benares on the Oude and Rohilkund Railway. The country, like the greater part of India, was as flat as a Western prairie, and the soil parched and dusty. For about six months of the year there is no rainfall whatever. At 7.30 P. M. I arrived at Lucknow. Pedro, my boy, got all my luggage together—for some was in the carriage with me and some in the van—and I drove to Hill's Imperial Hotel just in time for an eight-o'clock dinner.

On Sunday, January 17th, I went forth at an early hour with a Mohammedan guide and drove first to the Residency, which is a spot of deep interest to every Anglo-Saxon American as well as to Britons; for we Americans, being of the same race, take a kindred pride in the glorious deeds of England's soldiers. My guide had been in Lucknow at the time of the siege, and was one of the few

General view of Lucknow from the clock-tower.

natives who remained loyal. He pointed out the interesting spots; and an old soldier of the Eighty-fourth Regiment, who was one of the first relief party under Sir Henry Havelock, told me graphically the whole story of the Lucknow mutiny and relief. The suffering in mind and body of the brave garrison, surrounded by a horde of cruel and bloodthirsty foes, must have been great indeed; for they were fighting not only for their country and their lives, but for the honour of their wives and daughters. Lawrence, "who tried to do his duty," and Havelock, have gone down to history with enduring name as examples of Christian soldiers. I stood with reverent interest beside their graves. Sir James Outram and Lord Clive, better known as Sir Colin Campbell, received sepulture in Westminster Abbey, having

survived the privations and dangers of the mutiny and returned home to be honoured and rewarded.

I returned to the Imperial Hotel, took breakfast, and attended service at the English church, after which I drove to various points of interest, of which I may name the Kaiser-bagh, a former palace of the deposed King of Oude; the Jumma Musjid, or Great Mosque; the Great Imambara, a huge Mohammedan building with an adjoining mosque; the Husainabad Imambara, the tomb of King Sa'adat Ali Khan and Shot Najuf; the Chutter Munzil, or Umbrella Mansion, now used by the United Service Club; the Maitinière, a college founded by Major-General Claude Martin; the Dilkusha Palace; the Secunder Bagh, where two thousand Sepoys were bayonetted by the Ninety-third Highlanders and the Fifty-third Regiment; and the Alumbagh, where the heroic Havelock is buried.

At the Residency is a monument to the officers and men of the gallant Seventy-eighth (Mackenzie) Highlanders—the Ross-shire Buffs, now called the Seaforth Highlanders—whose bagpipes, according to tradition, were heard by Jessie Brown. The story is, that she was the first to know of the approach of Havelock's relieving force toward Lucknow. She was lying on the floor, sick with fever, her ear to the ground, when she suddenly leaped to her feet and declared that she heard the pipes of Havelock's Highland Brigade. As the fire continued to approach the commotion in the city became intense, while within the garrison all was exultation to know that, through God's mercy, deliverance was at hand, as foretold by the Scotch lassie in her delirium. The story is told in the following lines by Grace Campbell:

JESSIE'S DREAM.

"Far awa' to bonnie Scotland
   Has my spirit ta'en its flight,
An' I saw my mither spinnin'
   In our Highland hame at night;
I saw the kye a-browsin',
   My father at the plough,
And the grand auld hills aboon them a'—
   Wad I could see them now!

"O leddy, while upon your knees
   Ye held my sleepin' head,
I saw the little kirk at hame,
   Where Tam and I were wed;

The residency, Lucknow.

I heard the tune the pipers play'd,
  I kenn'd its rise and fa'
'Twas the wild Macgregor's slogan-
  'Tis the grandest o' them a'!

"Hark! sure I'm no wildly dreamin',
  For I hear it plainly now—
Ye cannot—ye never heard it
  On the far-off mountain's brow;
For in your southern childhood
  Ye were nourish'd saft and warm,
Nor watch'd upon the cauld hillside
  The risin' o' the storm!

"Ay! now the soldiers hear it,
  An' answer with a cheer,
As 'The Campbells are a-comin'!'
  Falls on each anxious ear!
The cannons roar their thunder,
  An' the sappers work in vain,
For high aboon the din o' war
  Resounds the welcome strain!

"An' nearer still, an' nearer still!
  An' now 'tis 'Auld Lang Syne!'
Its kindly notes like life-bluid rin
  Through this pair sad heart o' mine!
O leddy! dinna swoon awa'!
  Look up! the evil's past!
They're comin' now to dee wi' us,
  Or save us at the last!

"Then let us humbly, thankfully,
  Down on our knees and pray
For those who come through bluid and fire
  To rescue us this day;
That He may o'er them spread his shield,
  Stretch forth his arm, an' save
Bold Havelock an' his Highlanders,
  The bravest o' the brave!"

This incident has inspired two other poems that attained popularity because of the story—Robert Lowell's "Relief of Lucknow" and Whittier's "Pipes at Lucknow."

Lucknow is famous for its embroidery in gold thread, its silver jewellery, cotton goods, and pottery. The inhabitants smoke opium and eat *majoon*, otherwise called hasheesh, which is made from Indian hemp and is one of the most intoxicating agents known. The fuel

Mausoleum of King Sa'adat Ali Kahn, Lucknow.

generally used throughout India is cow-dung. This is pressed into round cakes and dried in the sun. It makes an excellent substitute for coal and wood, and burns much in the same manner as peat.

On Monday, January 18th, I drove about the environs of the town to the place of the military operations under the direction of the commander-in-chief, Sir Frederick Roberts. The troops, twelve thousand in all, were divided into two parties, one division defending and the other attacking Lucknow. The movements were well executed and very interesting, the English, native and volunteer regiments all taking part. These manœuvres occur yearly, and are intended not only for exercise and discipline, but to impress the natives — the charging, cannonading, and musketry firing being terrific. On the road I met about seventy camels and several hundred mules and bullocks belonging to the Government. They were splendid-looking animals, all in fine condition.

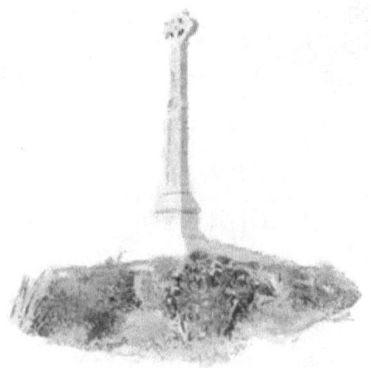

Monument to Sir Henry Lawrence, Lucknow

CHAPTER IX.

AGRA AND DELHI.

N the evening I left Lucknow for Cawnpore, forty-eight miles distant, and in two hours arrived at this historic city, the scene of the horrible massacre in June, 1857. I was met at the station by Joseph Lee, a former soldier of the Fifty-third or Shropshire Regiment, subsequently of the Twenty-third Regiment, Welsh Fusileers. He was one of the heroic band that entered Cawnpore with Havelock — unfortunately, two hours after the last of the English prisoners was killed by the mutineers under that barbarous murderer, Nana Sahib.

On Tuesday morning I went out in a large landau, the driver being an old soldier who also had served in the Fifty-third Regiment and entered Cawnpore with Havelock. The various spots of interest were shown—Wheeler's intrenchment, which had been distinctly marked out, at the suggestion of the Prince of Wales; All Soul's Church; the Memorial Well (into which the unfortunate English victims were thrown, regardless of age or sex, the living with the dead); and the Suttee Choura Ghât, where the majority of the garrison were fired upon

Memorial Building, Cawnpore, on the scene of the massacre of 1857.

and were destroyed, after they had embarked in boats. The massacre was one of the most brutal in modern history, but the retribution inflicted on the perpetrators was swift and heavy. They were dragged by Havelock's infuriated soldiers through the blood they had spilled, which to a Brahman's mind was an unspeakable defilement; and after that they were lashed to the mouths of cannon and the guns were fired, which blew their bodies into shreds and scattered them to the wind. The severity of this punishment arose from their religious belief, which requires that the body have burial with proper ceremonies or the soul can never enter heaven.

The guide informed me of a fact that is usually suppressed in the accounts of this tragedy. It seems that Sir Hugh Massey Wheeler had a native wife and four children—two sons and two daughters—and it is probable that this made him more ready to surrender than the other members of the garrison, the majority of whom would have preferred to hold out. General Wheeler, his wife, and one son were killed at the Ghât; the two daughters were taken by the rebel officers and dishonoured, and this was the fate also of many of the European ladies. One of Wheeler's daughters, so the story runs, seized the sword belonging to the man who had outraged her and ran him through with fatal effect. The other daughter is said to have remained voluntarily with the man who had appropriated her, though the mutiny was ended and an opportunity was given her to leave him. The remaining son afterward became a magistrate, and, strange to say, his feelings were all anti-English, and his decisions invariably favourable to the natives. Nana Sahib was well educated, and was a great favourite with the English ladies and gentlemen before the mutiny. He became disaffected toward the English rule because his right to the title and salute of Bajee Rao, who had adopted him as a son, was not recognized by the authorities.

I left Cawnpore on the 7.37 P. M. train, arriving at Agra at 4 A. M., and, as the night was fine and the moon shining, I sent Pedro to Laurie's Hotel with the luggage, took a *gharry*, and drove at once to see the Taj Mahal. The sight was one I shall never forget.

On Wednesday morning, January 20th, I engaged a native Hindu guide and spent the forenoon at Akbar's Tomb, which is six miles from Agra. This is a splendid construction of the Great Mogul whose tomb it forms. The view from the top story is beautiful. The Taj loomed up in the distance, and flocks of green parrots circled about in the air. Here, in the centre, is the memorial of Akbar, a large block of pure

Scene of the attempted escape from the massacre, 1857.

white marble, decorated with an Arabic inscription surrounded by exquisite tracery. A few feet from this monument is a marble receptacle in which was kept, it is said, the famous Koh-i-noor diamond—now one of the British crown jewels. In a dark chamber in the centre of this marvellous pile lie the crumbling remains of the mighty emperor.

In the afternoon I drove to the Taj Mahal. The gate through which we entered is in itself a marvel, and the view as one passes through it is sublime. I was ready to acknowledge without hesitation that, in spite of all that has been said in its praise, the first view of the Taj Mahal is not a disappointment. Its beauty is beyond description. The garden in which it is situated is filled with cypress, lemon, orange, and palm trees, and many flowering bushes and plants, while a tank about three hundred feet in length, filled with clear running water, extends through the middle.

It is remarkable how perfectly preserved the Taj Mahal is, when one considers that it was completed in 1648. The beautiful tracery and carving, as well as the intricate inlaid work, are almost as fresh as if it were just completed. Without doubt the Taj Mahal is the most exquisitely beautiful and the most perfect edifice in existence. Standing out in white relief against the cloudless azure sky, when the sun is sinking below the horizon, it is a sight never to be forgotten. The following description, by Sir Edwin Arnold, is probably the most beautiful as well as the most accurate that has been produced:

"The wonder of Agra, and the 'crown of the world,' the Taj, the peerless tomb built for the fair dead body of Arjamand Banu Begum by her lord and lover, the Emperor Shah Jehan—in truth, it is difficult to speak of what has been so often described, the charm of which remains nevertheless quite indescribable. As a matter of course, one's first hours in Agra were devoted to contemplation of that tender elegy in marble which, by its beauty, has made immortal the loveliness that it commemorates. The Tartar princes and princesses from which sprang the proud Lion of the Moguls were wont in their lifetime to choose a piece of picturesque ground, to inclose it with high walls, embellish its precincts with flower-beds and groves of shady trees, and to build upon it a Bari-duri, a 'twelve-gated' pleasure house, where they took delight during the founder's life. When he died, the pavilion became a mausoleum, and never again echoed with song and music. Perhaps the fair daughter of Asuf Khan, Shah Jehan's sultana, had loved this very garden in her life, for her remains were laid at death in its confines, while the emperor commissioned the

Interior of the Pearl Mosque, Agra.

best artificers of his time to build a resting-place for her dust worthy of the graces of mind and body which are recorded in the Persian verse upon her grave.

"In all the world no queen had ever such a monument. You have read a thousand times all about the Taj; you know exactly—so you believe—what to expect. There will be the gateway of red sandstone with the embroidered sentences upon it from the holy book; the demi-vault inlaid with flowers and scrolls; then the green garden opening a long vista over marble pavements between masses of heavy foliage, and mournful pillars of the cypress ranged like sentinels to guard the solemnity of the spot. At the far end of this vista, beyond the fountains and the marble platform, amid four stately white towers, you know what a sweet and symmetrical dome will be beheld, higher than its breadth, solid and majestic, but yet soft and delicate in its swelling proportions and its milk-white sheen. Prepared to admire, you are also aware of the defects alleged against the Taj—the rigidity of its outlines, the lack of shadow upon its unbroken front and flanks, and the coloured inlaying, said to make it less a triumph of architectural than of mosaic work—an illustration somewhat too striking and lavish of what is declared of the Moguls, that 'they designed like giants and finished like jewellers.' You determine to judge it dispassionately, not carried away by the remembrance that twenty thousand workmen were employed for twenty-two years in its construction; that it cost hard upon two million pounds sterling; that gems and precious stones came in camel-loads from all parts of the earth to furnish the inlayers with their material. Then you pass beneath the stately portal—in itself sufficient to commemorate the proudest of princesses—and as the white cupola of the Taj rises before the gaze and reveals its beauty, grace by grace, as you pace along the pavemented avenue, the mind refuses to criticise what enchants the eye and fills the heart with a sentiment of reverence for the royal love which could thus translate itself into alabaster. If it be the time of sunlight, the day is softened to perpetual afternoon by the shadows cast from the palms and peepuls, the thuja trees and the pomegranates, while the hot wind is cooled by the scent of roses and jasmine. If it be moonlight, the dark avenue leads the gaze mysteriously to the soft and lofty splendour of that dome. In either case, when the first platform is reached and the full glory of the snow-white wonder comes into light, one can no more stay to criticise its details than to analyze a beautiful face suddenly seen. Admiration, delight, astonishment, blend in the absorbed thought with a feeling that human affection never struggled more ardently, passionately, and triumphantly against the oblivion of death. There is one sustained, harmonious, majestic sorrowfulness of pride in it, from the verse on the entrance which says that "the pure of heart shall enter the Gardens of God," to the small delicate letters of sculptured Arabic upon the tombstone which tells with a refined humility that Mumtaz-i-Mahal, the 'Exalted of the Palace,' lies here, and that Allah alone is powerful.

"The garden helps the tomb as the tomb dignifies the garden. It is such an orderly wilderness of rich vegetation as could only be had in Asia, broad flags of banana belting the dark tangle of banyan and bamboo, with white pavements gleaming crosswise through the verdure. Yet, if the Taj rose amid sands of a dreary desert, the lovely edifice would beautify the waste and turn it into a tender parable of the desolation of death, and the power of love which is stronger than death. You pace around the four sides of the milk-white monument, pausing to observe the glorious prospect over the Indian plains commanded from the platform on that face where Jumna washes the foot of the wall. Its magnitude now astounds. The plinth of the Taj is over a hundred yards each way, and it lifts its golden pinnacle two hundred and forty-four feet into the sky. From a distance this lovely and aërial dome sits, therefore, above the horizon like a rounded cloud. And having paced about it, and saturated the mind with its extreme and irresistible loveliness, you enter reverently the burial-place of the Princess Arjamand, to find the inner walls of the monument as much a marvel of subtle shadow and chastened light, decked with delicate jewellery, as the exterior was noble and simple. On the pure surface of this hall of death, and upon the columns, panels, and trellis-work of the marble screens surrounding the tomb, are patiently inlaid all sorts of graceful and elaborate embellishments—flowers, leaves, berries, scrolls, and sentences—in jasper, coral, bloodstone, lapis-lazuli, nacre,

The Taj Mahal, Agra.

onyx, turquoise, sardonyx, and even precious gems. Moreover, the exquisite abode of death is haunted by spirits as delicate as their dwelling. They will not answer to rude noises, but if a woman's voice be gently raised in notes of hymn or song, if a chord is quietly sounded, echoes in the marble vault take up the music, repeat, diversify, and amplify it with strange combinations of melodious sounds, slowly dying away and rearising, as if Israfel, 'who has the sweetest voice of all Allah's angels,' had set a guard of his celestial minstrels to watch the death-couch of Arjamand. For under the beautiful screens and the carved trellis-work of alabaster is the real resting-place of the 'Exalted of the Palace.' She has the centre of the circular area marked by a little slab of snow-white marble; while by her side—a span loftier in height because he was a man and an emperor, but not displacing her from the pre-eminence of her grace and beauty—is the stone which marks the resting-spot of Shah Jehan, her lord and lover. He has immortalized, if he could not preserve alive for one brief day, his peerless wife; yet the pathetic moral of it all is written in a verse hereabouts from the *Hadees*, or 'traditions.' It runs, after reciting the styles and titles of 'His Majesty, King of Kings, Shadow of Allah, whose Court is as Heaven': *'Saith Jesus (on whom be peace): This world is a bridge! pass thou over it, but build not upon it. This world is one hour; give its minutes to thy prayers; for the rest is unseen.'*"

I left the Taj Mahal reluctantly, though knowing that I should have opportunities before leaving of seeing it again, and drove back to the fort. This is a huge mediæval structure of red sandstone, containing within its walls the beautiful Royal Palace. At the time this fortress was constructed it was impregnable, but against modern artillery, of course, it would not stand. The entrance is by the celebrated Delhi Gate, a massive structure, reached by a drawbridge over the moat. I drove through the fort to the beautiful Motee Masjid, or pearl mosque, built by Shah Jehan in 1654; to the Diwan-i-am, or public audience-hall, built by Aurungzebe in 1685, where the Prince of Wales held a famous public reception in 1875; to the wonderful Jasmine Tower; to the marvellous Shish Mahal, or Oriental bath, the walls and ceilings of which are ornamented with countless small bits of looking-glass, arranged in curious designs; and to other parts of this grand habita-

tion of the Great Moguls. Lord Northbrook has defrayed the cost of some necessary restoration, for which he deserves the thanks of every visitor interested in the preservation of Indian antiquities.

The Jasmine Tower was a boudoir of the chief sultana. The terrace is paved with gray and white marbles, laid out for the game of *pachisi*, similar to our draughts or checkers, on a grand scale. Ascending a few steps, you enter a marble pavilion two stories high, built on a circular bastion facing the river.

On Thursday, January 21st, I revisited the various places of interest and took a more deliberate and critical view. For several hours I tarried at the Taj, remaining there until the waning sunlight warned me that night would soon set in. Each successive visit to this masterpiece of Mohammedan architecture increases one's admiration for its wonderful beauty.

Many elegant articles are manufactured in Agra, and one need not go off the hotel piazza to purchase them, although a visit to the Bazar is of considerable interest. In this the specimens of embroideries on French satin, in gold and silver thread, with inserted coloured stones, are magnificent. They are made for European uses, in such forms as portières, bed-spreads, doilies, and centre-pieces for dining-tables, and are produced in particular by the factory of Ganash, Lall & Son. This firm has a large trade with the nobility and gentry of England.

On Friday morning, January 22d, I left for Delhi, with my servant Pedro. At the station I had a discussion with the station-master about taking my luggage into the first-class carriage, but the matter ended most pleasantly, for when he found I was an American he permitted me to have my way. He said he had lived formerly in Chicago, and was there at the time of the great fire.

A Nautch girl.

The country through which we passed was devoted almost entirely to raising wheat, but near Agra large quantities of cotton are also produced. The windows of the carriages on the Indian railways are usually made of blue glass, which is useful in fending off the glare and heat of the sun in the hot months.

Almost every writer seems to have his own method of spelling not only the Hindu names, but also other words not entirely relating to India, which is exasperatingly confusing. The poor tourist on his way round the world is in danger of softening of the brain should he dip too deeply into the history and geography of the places he beholds.

We arrived at Delhi at 4 P. M., and went to the Grand Hotel. In the evening I witnessed a fine performance of Nautch girls. These dancers are employed by the rajahs and rich Hindus to entertain the guests at weddings, festivals, and other celebrations. I was with a fellow-traveller, we being the only lookers-on. There were four girls, richly costumed, and covered with native jewellery—necklaces, nose rings, finger rings, and toe rings, and bangles on arms and ankles, besides other ornaments. The bangles on the ankles were covered with tiny bells, the tinkling of which made a pleasant accompaniment to the music produced by eight performers playing on native violins and tom-toms. The dances were graceful and modest, and I was much interested in the entertainment. The whole cost for the four Nautch girls and eight musicians was sixty rupees.

On Saturday I engaged a local native guide, and, setting out at 7 A. M., drove in a large open landau to the fort, inside of which is the palace of the Great Mogul. This resembles in a general way the fort and palace of Agra; in fact, many other buildings in Delhi bear the same resemblance, having been constructed principally by Akbar and Shah Jehan. This edifice was begun in A. D. 1628, and completed in 1658 by Shah Jehan. At that time it was undoubtedly the most sumptuous and magnificent palace existing. The Diwan-i-am, or public audience hall, is a beautiful building, of red sandstone inlaid with white marble. In the centre is the imperial throne, covered by a canopy of white marble, beautifully decorated. Directly on the outer wall, beside the river Jumna, are the Motee Musjid, the richly decorated baths of Akbar, and the Diwan-i-knas, a private audience hall, the ceiling of which was originally of solid silver. In the centre of the exquisitely beautiful chamber is the marble pedestal on which formerly stood that wonder of the world, the Peacock Throne. The plumage of the peacocks was composed of sapphires, diamonds, rubies, emeralds, and other precious stones, the tails of the birds being spread. At the back of the throne was a parrot, life size, said to have been cut from a single emerald; while on either side of the throne stood an umbrella, one of the Oriental emblems of royalty, made of crimson velvet, embroidered heavily with superb fringe composed of pearls.

Pearl Mosque in fort, Delhi.

Each handle, eight feet in length, was of solid gold, thickly studded with the finest diamonds.

This throne, it is said, cost six million pounds sterling, when jewels were not valued so highly as at present. On the north wall is an inscription in Persian letters, the meaning of which is, "If there be an elysium on earth, it is this—it is this!" The other buildings remaining of the palace are all in harmony with one another, and the Motee Musjid is especially lovely.

My next visit was to the Jama Masjid. Here some highly interesting relics were shown me; namely, a slipper of Mohammed's, a hair from his beard, and his footprint in a piece of marble, besides several ancient and rare copies of the Koran. These articles are looked upon with great veneration by all good Mussulmans. The view of Delhi from the minarets of this mosque is fine.

After this I returned for breakfast, and then continued my sight-seeing to the Cashmere Gate, through which the British troops entered after its demolition by a mine of gunpowder in 1857; to the Mutiny Memorial on the ridge; then through the Delhi Gate, viewing the great Stone Pillar; to the ruined city of Ferozeshah; to Humayoon's tomb, where Major Hodson captured and executed the two sons of the last Mogul; to Nizam-ood-Deen's tomb; and to Indraprestha. All these places are of the greatest interest. Many of the ruined buildings along the roadside were constructed as long ago as 2000 B.C.; for Delhi was a great capital when Babylon and Nineveh were flourishing.

Coming back, I spent some time in the bazaars. No other city in India produces such choice articles, in such large quantities, as does the famous capital of the Moguls. This day was the most interesting one that I spent in India. The romance attaching to the place, its early history, its Oriental grandeur under the Moguls, its capture by Lord Lake in 1803, and its second capture and seizure by the British under General Nicholson in 1857, and the facts of the final extinction of the old *régime*, together with Hodson's remarkable exploit in capturing the last of the Moguls with a mere handful of horsemen, and his shooting the two princes, heirs to the throne, and exposing their bodies to public view—all invest Delhi with a peculiar interest.

The principal streets are wide, and are macadamized in English style. The main thoroughfare, called Chandnee Chowk, is a mile long, and one hundred and twenty feet broad, and is planted in the middle with a double line of trees, after the fashion of Unter-den-Linden.

There are but few Hindu temples in Delhi, and those are of no special interest. The Jain Temple is open each day in the afternoon, and I drove thither. It resembles the ordinary Buddhist shrines. In the evening, before going to bed, I took a Turkish bath, there being an excellent establishment at Delhi.

In India there are no old maids or old bachelors; for it is the duty, taught by his religion, of every parent to provide a husband or a wife, as the case may be, for his children when they are about seven years of age. One often sees in the streets the wedding processions of these youthful couples. Of course, they do not live together at once, but continue with their families until they are of proper age.

On Sunday, January 24th, I attended service at St. James's Church, which is a commodious edifice in a beautiful compound near the hotel. Afterward I drove out eleven miles to Kootub-Minar, stopping on the way to see the tomb of Sufder Jung. Nearly the whole distance from the Ajmere Gate shows a succession of ruined towns, tombs, and mosques. Kootub-Minar was a glorious surprise to me, for, next to the Taj, it is the principal architectural sight of India. Its height is two hundred and thirty-eight feet, the diameter at the base being forty-seven feet, and at the top nine feet. The carvings of the beautifully fluted outer walls are as fresh as if they had been cut but a score of years. It is the third highest tower in the world, and was completed six hundred and fifty years ago—a fact difficult to realize when one stands at its base and looks up at it. The ruined buildings surrounding the tower were originally Hindu temples, but were reconstructed into mosques, retaining, however, the original carved pillars, which have an unusual look in a Mohammedan house of worship. In the centre of the courtyard is an ancient iron column supposed to date from A. D. 400. It rises twenty-two feet above ground, and extends three feet below the surface. It is considered to be one of the most curious things at Delhi.

Near Kootub-Minar is a pleasant-looking dak bungalow for the accommodation of such travellers as wish to remain for a few days to make a more thorough examination of these interesting relics of bygone generations.

Returning to Laurie's Hotel, I stopped to see the Jama Masjid, or Friday Mosque, which faces the entrance to the fort. It stands on a plateau of rock, which is approached by four streets on the four sides. The gates are reached by flights of broad stone steps. The courtyard, four hundred and fifty feet square, is surrounded by cloisters, the roofs of which are of sandstone slabs fifteen feet long, while the court itself is paved with granite and marble. The mosque, at one side of the yard, is two hundred and sixty feet long and one hundred and twenty feet wide, and is the finest in the world. It is constructed of red sandstone, inlaid with white marble, and its central arch is eighty feet high. The domes are of white marble, and the minarets of marble and sandstone in alternate stripes. The floor is mainly of white marble, and each slab in it, three feet long and a foot and a half wide, surrounded by a black border, is occupied by one worshipper on Friday.

On Monday, January 25th, I left Delhi at 11 A. M. by the Rajpootana-Malwa Railroad, a metre-gauge line, for Jeypore, arriving at the latter place at 10.45 P. M. The country through which we passed was well cultivated and fertile, the principal crops being cotton and wheat. The land is flat, save for disconnected hills here and there. On the top of many are castles, somewhat like those on the Rhine. Along the way I saw large flocks of wild peacocks, doves, partridges, pigeons, and snipes, besides an occasional antelope. For a change, instead of going to the Kaiser-i-Hind Hotel, I put up at the dak bungalow, and found it very comfortable. Jeypore is the capital of an independent principality and is the largest city of the Rajpootana states. It is governed by a maharajah, the present ruler being an enlightened, progressive man. He has his own army, and administers his own government, independent of British influence, so long as the Resident does not object. The population numbers perhaps two million, composed of Rajpoots and other Hindus, Mohammedans, and Jains. The army consists of about twenty thousand troops, but to judge from appearance is not very effective. The city is pleasantly situated in a valley surrounded by high hills, the tops of which in many instances are surmounted by picturesque castellated forts, the largest one, called Tiger Fort, completely commanding the town. A substantial wall, twenty feet high and nine feet thick, surrounds the city, communication being had with the neighbouring country by means of gateways. The streets of Jeypore

Maharajah of Jeypore

Sun procession day, Fyzpore.

are wide, hard, and clean, and the houses well built of brick and stucco.

On Tuesday, January 26th, I first visited the Ramniwas Garden, which is beautifully laid out and well cared for; it would be a credit to any European city. Here is a fine zoölogical collection, remarkably well arranged, the animals, especially the tigers, being magnificent, and their cages of the newest and most approved pattern. I have never seen a zoölogical garden so free from disagreeable odours,

Palace of the Winds, Jeypore.

and I should say that the management was superior to that of any other, not excepting Regent's Park. In the Public Garden there is also an exceptionally handsome museum, called Albert Hall, the finest new building in all India, which contains an interesting collection of objects illustrative of Indian manufactures and arts.

I then went to the alligator tank, a basin of water about an acre in extent. On the way my guide bought some goat's flesh, and when we arrived there the keeper attached the meat to a rope, and then

Elephant with cat trappings, Jeypore.

called to the alligators, which were sleeping at the farther corner of the tank. They soon heard his voice and understood the meaning of the call. It was curious to see them, in the distance, first raise their unsightly heads to listen, then crawl down the bank, plunge into the water, and swim rapidly in our direction. A half dozen enormous ones were soon struggling with each other to secure the food offered them. After this we were shown through the palace, and viewed the exterior of the Hawal Mahal, or Hall of the Winds, which is the part of the palace where the maharajah's wives reside. Great preparations were in progress for the marriage of his Highness, which took place a week later. Triumphal arches were in process of erection, and the streets were receiving a decoration of flags and coloured poles. I was informed that the maharajah had already five wives, but no offspring, and that he was about to complete the half dozen in hopes that the last union would be fruitful.

I then returned to luncheon, and spent the afternoon in driving through the streets and visiting shops and bazaars. Just before dark the scene in the market place, outside the city walls, was the most characteristically Oriental spectacle that I can remember. It was a Mussulman festival, and the market place was crowded with people dressed in their gayest costumes. The Mohammedan women wore trousers of a red cotton material, tight at the ankles, and baggy from the knee to the hips; while the Hindu women's costume was a skirt and a small jacket, if it could be thus designated, which extended only halfway to the elbow, and covered the upper part of the bust, leaving a wide space of their stomachs uncovered. The women of each class had a long piece of cotton cloth over the head and extending to the knees, which they wore gracefully adjusted round their persons. As usual, all these women were covered, so to speak, with native jewellery and ornaments.

Many elephants and magnificent horses from the maharajah's stables were mixed up with the masses of human beings, while trains of camels wound their way along, carrying loads to far-distant places. As we were looking on at this curious gathering, suddenly through the city gate several carriages made their appearance, containing some native princes escorted by a guard of mounted spearmen, and the crowd fell back in haste to make a passage for the party.

There are several pleasant excursions to be made from Jeypore: one to the Temple of the Sun, and another to the Sanganer Temple, which contains some peculiarly carved figures of native gods. But the principal attraction outside of Jeypore is the ancient but now deserted city of Ambar.

Throughout India the different districts have their specialties in manufactures, and Jeypore has a world-wide reputation for the excellence of its enamelling.

Fragment of temple at Jeypore.

The palace at Ambar.

CHAPTER X.

IN WESTERN INDIA AND EGYPT.

WEDNESDAY, January 27th, I took an early start for Ambar, passing through the city and driving out about four miles farther, where the elephant which had been sent by the maharajah's orders was waiting, and I at once "transferred" from the carriage to his back. He was a huge animal, with fine tusks, and was covered with handsome red trappings. In an hour we reached the deserted city of Ambar, an interesting place, strongly fortified, and surrounded by a stone wall, in which at regular intervals are small towers. A troop of large, long-tailed monkeys — wild, of course — were running over the housetops or jumping in the branches of the trees, and as we passed close to them they made ugly grimaces at us.

We dismounted, and went first to the temple of the horrible, bloodthirsty Kali, at whose shrine a goat is killed each morning. The blood of the morning's sacrifice was still fresh on the pavement, and the sword used by the priest was ready in its place for the next victim to be decapitated. At certain festivals the temple resembles a slaughter-house, for large numbers of sheep and buffaloes are also offered up to the sanguinary deity.

I was then shown through the palace, which contains many fine rooms. Some of them are ornamented with small bits of mica and looking-glasses set in the walls and ceilings. The view from the windows is exceedingly picturesque; the surrounding hills are crowned with castles, and there is a beautiful green valley in the distance.

By two o'clock I was again at the dak bungalow. In the afternoon I drove out seven miles to the Sanganer Temple. This is very old, and quite unlike anything that I had seen. It contains a number of marble idols, some white and some black. After dinner I took the night train for Ahmedabad, it being impossible to begin the trip by daylight.

The Rajah of Rutlam.

On Thursday, January 28th, I spent the day on the train. I was very comfortable on the journey, having taken the precaution to reserve the whole compartment. Along the route we passed many fields of grain of different kinds, poppies, and castor-oil plants. I was surprised to see hundreds of apes and many adjutant-birds, some of which were nearly as large as an ostrich, quite near the railway. All wild animals and birds in India are remarkably tame, as they are never disturbed by the natives. Arriving at Ahmedabad at 6.30 P. M., I slept in one of the rooms provided for travellers in the railway station, there being no hotel there.

Ahmedabad is the principal city of the province of Guzerat, and is considered one of the most picturesque cities in India. It is on the banks of Sabarmati River. The town is surrounded by a high wall pierced by fourteen gateways, whose strong, spike-studded doors of teak are worthy of examination. These walls were built previous to 1443 by Ahmed Shah.

Architecturally Ahmedabad is one of the most interesting cities of the East. Two centuries ago it was one of the finest in India, but it was ruined in the Mahratta wars. When it was conquered by the Mussulmans the high civilization of its inhabitants so far influenced the invaders that the temples continued to be built largely in Indo-Saracenic style, though with adaptation to the change from Hindu to Mohammedan requirements. The mosques have minarets and ornamentation of wonderful richness. The city is filled with beautiful specimens of carving on the doors, windows, and verandas of the houses, which usually are made of teak wood.

I was greatly delighted with the beautiful architecture and carving that I saw, especially at the Jumma Musjid, the Rani Asni, the Sidi Syed Shah Alams, the Queen's mosques, and the magnificent shrine of Hathi Sing, a Jain temple dedicated to Dharmanath. Dada Hari's Well is unique, certainly wholly unlike anything I had previously seen. Steps lead down beneath the ground from portico to portico, ending in great pillared galleries, and these are all richly carved through a length of a hundred and fifty feet. Thirty feet below the surface is a circular well, which is also surrounded by elaborately carved pillars, with cool retreats from the burning sun and sand.

The Pinjapol, a large hospital for sick animals, covers three acres. It is filled with cages, sheds, and pens, in which disabled, sick, and aged animals are taken care of. There is a room reserved for vermin taken off the persons of very punctilious Hindus who do not wish to kill even a louse or a flea. These are taken to the Pinjapol, where they are fed on the bodies of men hired for that purpose.

At 7.30 P. M. I left on the Bombay, Baroda, and Central India

Colonel Elphinstone and the author on the Maharajah's elephant.

Railway. Through the courtesy of the station-master, a first-class compartment had been reserved for me and a fellow-passenger whom I had met on the Rosetta, without extra charge. The train was the fastest and best in every respect that I travelled on in India.

On Saturday morning, at 7.30, I arrived at Bombay, and was met at Church Gate Station by a porter and drove at once to the Esplanade Hotel, whither I had telegraphed for rooms. I rested until the afternoon, when I drove to the Towers of Silence, belonging to the Parsees. These towers, five in number, are on Malabar Hill, surrounded by a beautiful garden. The view of the city, the sea, and the neighbouring bungalows is one of the finest in Bombay. Perched on the top of the towers are usually a number of vultures waiting for the approach of a funeral. The procession stops near the tower; only the bearers of the corpse enter with the body,

The late Maharana of Oodeypore.

and lay it, with all its clothing removed, upon the tower's top. On their retirement the vultures immediately descend, and in a few minutes devour the flesh, leaving only the bones, which are thrown into a central pit of the tower, to resolve themselves into dust and ashes.

The Parsees were originally inhabitants of Persia, but were driven from their native country twelve hundred years ago, and nearly all are now living in Bombay, where many of them have acquired great wealth. Their peculiar hat was a novelty to me, as I had seen but few of them before. The name Bombay is derived from Bombaim or Mombaim, a corruption of Mumbader, the name of a Hindu goddess whose shrine was there. The Portuguese took possession of the island in 1529, and in 1661 it was ceded to Charles II of England as a part of the dowry of his wife, Catherine of Braganza. Since that time it

A Tower of Silence, Bombay

has remained under British rule. The city is decidedly the handsomest in India, but it does not afford the social advantages of Calcutta with its vice-regal court. The public buildings are exceptionally fine. The new station of the Great Peninsular Railway is probably the finest in existence. Bombay is the second cotton port in the world, being next in importance to New Orleans. There are many cotton mills, the greater number owned by Parsees. These were constructed between 1861 and 1865, during the war in the United States, when, on account of the blockade of the Southern ports, all supplies from that region ceased.

Just before sunset the Apollo Bunder is a delightful spot, commanding a view of the harbour and shipping. Here is the Yacht Club, to which I was invited as a visitor. The Government House is at the extremity of Malabar Hill, very near the seashore.

The population of Bombay is about 800,000 persons, only five per cent. of whom are Christians, including Europeans and Eurasians. This hardly speaks well for the proselytizing power of the missionaries, who have laboured there for several hundred years.

On Sunday, January 31st, I visited the Crawford Market, which is in a handsome building and well conducted. The display of tropical fruits, grains, and vegetables, as well as the fish and live birds, I found highly interesting. After seeing this, I attended St. Thomas's Cathedral, a large edifice, with many handsome mural monuments. The service was decidedly High Church.

I had received a polite invitation from two native gentlemen to spend several weeks with them shooting tigers and wild elephants, but after deliberation I concluded that I would not postpone my departure, as the voyage to the Red Sea would be uncomfortable later in the season. Sunday afternoon I drove for two hours, and enjoyed the cool breezes from the Arabian Sea.

On Monday, February 1st, at 3 P. M., I embarked on a small launch belonging to the Esplanade Hotel, at the Apollo Bunder. After a charming sail along the water front, and threading the mass of native boats congregated near the shore, we arrived in an hour at the beautiful island where the Caves of Elephanta are. The tide being out, the launch was moored, and the passengers went ashore in a small boat. We were landed on a narrow breakwater made of detached blocks of concrete. A number of steps — one hundred and twenty, I believe — had to be mounted, and then we arrived at the cottage of the custodian. He came out to meet us, and proved to be an old soldier. We purchased tickets—for the Government compels every one to do this—at two annas each (equivalent to four cents), and were then escorted into the cave, the custodian describing it to us. The cavern is hewn out of the solid rock, and it is certainly wonderful with what skill the columns and figures are made, when the tools that the builders used are considered. It seemed to be principally devoted to Siva, the destroying god, and in two separate rooms are mammoth emblems of that disgusting deity—the male and female organs of generation. The return trip was delightful, and we reached the stairs at the Apollo Bunder just as the sun was setting. The whole space was crowded with people listening to a band that was playing in the grounds of the Yacht Club.

Tuesday, Wednesday, Thursday, and Friday were spent in shopping; in daily visits to the Back Bay swimming-bath, which is one of the best institutions of its kind that I have seen; and in driving, and listening to the military band each afternoon. The climate is pleasant and salubrious, the mornings and evenings being cool, with a light breeze. In the middle of the day the sun was hot, but not uncomfortably so, and at all times the air was invigorating and brisk.

The servants in Bombay, as in every other part of India, never wear stockings or shoes. This is true of men and women in private families, as well as of those employed at clubs and hotels. In large dining-rooms, like those in the great Eastern Hotel at Calcutta and the Esplanade Hotel at Bombay, this fact prevents a great deal of noise and confusion, as no footsteps are heard. In the United States, at the large hotels in Saratoga, Newport, and St. Augustine, the heavy tread and squeaking boots of the Irish and negro waiters, together with the clatter they make with the dishes, are sometimes almost deafening. Should I again go to Bombay I would take up my quarters at the Byculla Club.

I was agreeably surprised to meet in Bombay a gentleman and his wife who had been fellow-travellers with me several years before in Yucatan. One never knows where he may next meet his friends, for in these days of electricity and steam the world is comparatively small.

Entrance to the Caves of Elephanta.

Saturday, February 6th, at noon, I left the stairs at the Apollo Bunder in a steam launch, was conveyed on board the steamer that should take me to Aden, and said farewell to the great Indian Empire. My recollections of India will ever be pleasant, although I did not depart with the same keen regret as when I sailed away from Japan. However, I certainly left with the best wishes for the wonderful country whose population is composed of so many races, creeds, and castes, and I was firmly convinced that the government which Great Britain has given to the natives is the best one possible for them. As they become fitted by education, they are gradually acquiring more voice in the direction of public affairs; while in the offices under the Government, and in those of the railways and banks and in the counting-rooms of many merchants, they are supplanting European employees, since they perform the same work for less wages.

The absurdity of caste restrictions is becoming apparent to those natives who have obtained a liberal education, and many eminent Brahman barristers have ceased to care whether they are in caste or out of it; while others, who do not wish to take the final step of separation, realize fully how foolish are the old ideas and restrictions.

Two things are essential for Indian prosperity: First, the higher education of women and their emancipation from compulsory marriage. They should be allowed to consult their own wishes, and to remain single as long as they prefer that condition, instead of being driven into early marriage and bearing children while they are children themselves. Second, the remonetization of silver and the fixing of a ratio between silver and gold. This is a most vital matter, for the present fluctuations are disastrous to trade and enterprise. Britain has been blind, in these respects, to the interests of her own land as well as of her Asiatic possessions. At present, however, taken for all in all, she is conscientiously doing her best to give India a good government, and protection to life and property is nearly as well assured as in England itself, if not more so; and there is much less crime, I am ashamed to admit, in India than in our own great republic.

The extension of railways is going on steadily, and prevents the occurrence of famine. All up-country towns will have their waterworks before long; and modern sanitary regulations are constantly introduced into city and village, sometimes against the wishes of the ignorant.

Once more I found myself on board a Peninsular and Oriental steamer, this time the Siam, of 3,050 tons, Captain H. T. Weighell, bound for Aden. At 2 p.m. on Saturday, February 6th, we hoisted our anchor and sailed out of the harbour of Bombay, and soon the shore of India faded from our view. The first luncheon I enjoyed very much, it being an agreeable change from the wretched food supplied at the Indian hotels, which are mostly very poor, the Great Eastern at Calcutta and the Esplanade at Bombay being especially dirty and badly managed.

The voyage was an ideal one, the Arabian Sea being as smooth as the Hudson River in summer, the weather fine, the air of just a pleasant temperature, and the silvery moonlight shining every night. On Thursday morning when I awoke we were skirting the shore of Arabia, and at six o'clock we arrived at Aden.

Aden is on a barren, rocky peninsula ten miles long and three miles wide. The population of the British territory governed by the political resident is about 35,000. Water is very scarce there, as it rains only once in about three years. This difficulty is somewhat obviated by storing water in huge tanks constructed many centuries ago, of solid masonry, where a supply for several years can be kept; and now a condensing apparatus furnishes the shipping with all the water necessary.

A strong garrison is maintained at Aden, notwithstanding the unhealthfulness and heat of the place, for it guards the road to India, and is second only to Gibraltar in importance. The houses of the natives are built usually of bamboo, and placed in the sand in a peculiar way. There is a breed of sheep indigenous to this neighbourhood which have large, fat tails weighing a dozen pounds or more, and make excellent mutton.

Railway station, Bombay.

The Sultan of Lahej was formerly the ruler of Aden, and frequently made himself objectionable by plundering English ships, so that in 1839 the East India Company found it necessary to send a force to punish him. After a sharp fight the place was captured, and it has remained ever since under the British flag. The opening of the Suez Canal gave Aden great importance both as a coaling-station and as a protection to commerce.

As we approached the town we saw lying at anchor, besides several war ships, the two Peninsular and Oriental boats that were to connect with the Siam, viz., the Cathay for Marseilles, and the Britannia, of 6,257 tons, Captain Julius Orman, R. N. R., for Brindisi, the latter being the ship to which I was transferred. She is one of the Jubilee boats, the finest in the service.

Soon after casting anchor we were taken on a tender, with our luggage, and sent over to the Britannia, everything being conducted without confusion or noise. The scene, when we went on board, was quite different from anything I had witnessed on shipboard. It was the dinner hour, and the passengers — both ladies and gentlemen — were dressed in evening costume. The ship is beautifully decorated, and has splendid wide decks, the effect being like that of the veranda of a summer hotel at the seaside. The passengers were mostly Australians, who are quite a different people from native-born Britons.

At 10 P. M. we left Aden, the full moon shining and not a ripple on the water, and passed through the Strait of Bab-el-Mandeb into the Red Sea during the night.

The weather remained pleasant, becoming cooler as we pursued our way northward; and the water was as tranquil as the traditional mill-pond. Each day we passed steamers, and occasionally we saw some barren, uninhabited islands. Most of the passengers had been on board for nearly a month, and were very sociable and friendly. Concerts, literary entertainments, and athletic sports followed one another almost daily, and relieved somewhat the monotony of the voyage.

There were several particularly handsome young Australian ladies, tall, stalwart, and smart in appearance, and with an ease of manner more American than English. There were also several Americans aboard, and I was much struck with the shrill twang of the ladies' voices as compared with the Australians'. I remember going to Newport with Monsignor Capel, when he was in favor with the "highlifers" at that fashionable resort—of course before he fell into disrepute—and when asked what American peculiarity he had especially noticed, he answered without hesitation, "The high-pitched voices of your women, which at a kettledrum or reception become a nasal shriek." This unfortunately is true, and I am sorry to say that it is more evident among the women than among the men of our country. I do not advocate copying the English pronunciation, for a nation with a population of sixty-five million has certainly a right to pronounce, spell, and speak as it chooses, without regard to what other nations may do; but what an improvement it would be if we modulated our voices as the Italians do, and enunciated our words with a musical intonation—"an excellent thing in woman"! This would be a good theme for one of Ward McAllister's Chesterfieldian letters. In matters of this kind the dictum of a leader of society might work a change where the proclamation of the Chief Magistrate, if such a thing were possible, would be ineffectual.

On Saturday, February 13th, we passed Jeddah, the port of Mecca, but at a considerable distance, and Sunday night, at nine o'clock, our voyage through the Red Sea was ended, for at that time our good ship entered the narrow Gulf of Suez. Here, on our right, was Mount Sinai, which is not a solitary peak, as it is generally supposed to be, but rather a group of mountains. The spot is pointed out where, according to tradition, Moses received the Ten Commandments. It is now called Jebel Moosa, and is perhaps seven thousand feet above the sea.

Early on Monday morning we approached Suez, the entrance to that marvel of modern engineering which connects the waters of Europe and Asia. Canals were cut there in ancient times, and Napoleon Bonaparte had a plan for one which he did not have the opportunity of executing. The honour of carrying to completion the project of the present canal belongs entirely to the ability and energy of Ferdinand de Lesseps, who spent the best part of his life in the development of the enterprise, which he successfully finished, although many of the best English engineers considered it not feasible. The total original cost of the Suez Canal was about twenty millions sterling. At first it was not profitable, but it was used more each year, until now it is paying well. One of the most brilliant acts of Lord Beaconsfield's government, in 1876, was the acquisition by England, for four million pounds, of the Egyptian interest in the canal; for in 1894, when these shares will receive their full rights again, the value will be fully three times the original cost, England having had five per cent. interest yearly. From Suez to Port Said the distance is eighty-seven miles, Ismailia being about halfway.

An Egyptian rider

The width of the canal channel for deep vessels is seventy-two feet, the whole distance; and at frequent intervals are *gares*, or sidings, to enable ships to pass one another. The electric light now used on steamers makes it possible for them to go through by night with the same facility as by day. By the official tables, in 1860, 2,522 ships of Great Britain, of a gross tonnage of 7,438,682 tons, passed through the canal, to three United States ships of a gross tonnage of 2,112 tons. These are figures on which it would be well for the Solons of our national legislature to reflect, with a view to discovering some means of creating a mercantile marine for the United States.

At the Bitter Lakes, traversed by the canal, the supposed spot is pointed out at which the children of Israel made their miraculous passage, where the hosts of Pharaoh were swallowed up.

In appearance the canal is like a large ditch, the banks being rough and without vegetation, as it passes only through the desert. We set out from Suez at 9 A. M., but unfortunately, about three hours later, our ship ran ashore on the west side and remained there, blocking the canal until 4.30 P. M. Vessels of the size of the Britannia rarely succeed in making the passage without a delay of this kind, which could be avoided by increasing the width of the channel a little. This widening, of course, would be expensive, but the benefits to commerce therefrom would be so great that I have no doubt it will soon be effected. We were detained a second time at the Bitter Lakes, and anchored for two hours, arriving at Ismaïlia at 11 P. M.

The passage through the canal at night is very beautiful and brilliant. The powerful search-light at the bow of the ship illuminates not only the water way but also both banks, giving a peculiarly weird look to the surroundings, making the shore appear like snow, and the white buoys by which the channel is marked seem to be of transparent glass. The green and red gasoline beacons add to the strangeness of the scene.

We passengers were taken on board a tender and brought without incident to the shore, whence I went to the Victoria Hotel, kept in French style, and there slept comfortably, although not luxuriously. The next morning my luggage was passed by the customs, and at 12.40 I left for Cairo on the railway, passing on the way the battle-field of Tel-el-Kebir. The breastworks thrown up by the English are distinctly seen, and near the station is the little cemetery in which are interred the brave fellows who fell. Here the army of Arabi Pasha was defeated and his power in Egypt terminated. The action of England at this time casts one of the greatest stains on her record, and stands out prominent among the many instances of

Bedouin sheik from the neighbourhood of Ghaza.

her brutality and her bullying of weaker nations. The interference in Egyptian affairs was in reality in behalf of the bondholders who had foolishly loaned their money to a spendthrift Khedive. The bombardment of Alexandria was inexcusable; the subsequent occupation of the country, and the piling on of taxes to pay the debt held by foreigners, was unjust to the poor Egyptian fellahs, and an insult to

Shepheard's hotel, Cairo.

the Sultan of Turkey, from whom the Khedive derives his authority. But good sometimes arises out of evil, and the government, since it came under the direction of Sir Evelyn Baring — for he is the real ruler — has been improved in every department; and for the young Khedive who has just succeeded the prospects are very bright.

At Ismailia I was delighted with the climate, cool and bracing, with continuous sunshine. Nothing can be finer than Egypt in winter. For some distance after leaving Ismailia the train passes through the desert, but after a little time it enters the fertile district irrigated from the Nile, and the contrast between the dreary waste of sand and the green fields is most striking.

View on the Nile.

As I approached Cairo the great pyramids loomed up in the distance. At 5 P. M. I arrived, and took a carriage to Shepheard's Hotel, where I found a room reserved for me, for which I had telegraphed for this is the favourite hotel, and it is difficult to get accommodations. What a change it was! I felt as if I were once more in the domain of civilization. All the appointments were good, and the table d'hôte dinner, to which every one goes, was excellent.

Base of the Great Pyramid.

On Wednesday, February 17th, I secured the services of an Arab guide named Hassan Wyse, and drove first to the great museum at Ghizeh and spent some time in looking at its fine collection, which illustrates the ancient history of the country. Many mummies that have been identified as those of the former kings are shown in an almost perfect state of preservation, besides other interesting objects. I continued then to the pyramids, over an excellent road lined with large shade trees, a road constructed prior to the visit of the Prince of Wales in 1868. I stopped at the Mena House, an excellent hotel within ten minutes' walk of the Great Pyramid of Cheops. Here, at one o'clock, I had my breakfast, and afterwards went to the top, and into the interior chamber of the pyramid. The ascent to the apex is difficult, but with the assistance of two stout Arab lads I accomplished it without much fatigue. Having finished the inspection of Cheops, I mounted a camel and rode over to the Sphinx, which is about a quarter of a mile away. The Sphinx was in existence when the Great Pyramid was built. Its body is cut from the natural rock —in place, as a geologist would say—the defects here and there being filled out with mason-work. The head is carved out completely. What divinity was worshipped in the sanctuary between its paws, is a riddle for the Sphinx to answer.

At a little distance the Great Pyramid does not seem so high as it is. One does not fully realize its size until he stands at its base and looks up. Sir Gardner Wilkinson gives the dimensions as follows: Base line, 732 feet; height, 460 feet; area of base, 535,824 square feet. If it were to be set down in Union Square, New York, there would be room for it on the north-and-south line, but some buildings would have to be cut away on the east or west side; and its apex would be three times as high as the loftiest building that fronts the square.

Returning, I stopped to see the Palace of Gezeereh, which is built directly on the banks of the Nile, opposite Boolak. There is a neatly laid-out garden attached to it, and the palace interior itself is very handsome. When I arrived at the hotel again, I felt tired but not exhausted, for the air is full of ozone.

"He who has not seen Cairo has not seen the world," says the Jewish physician in The Story of the Humpback; "its soil is gold, its Nile is a wonder; its women are like the black-eyed virgins of paradise." Cairo is certainly, as a residence, the most attractive of Oriental cities, combining all the luxuries of Western civilization with the ancient Mohammedan customs and habits. The new part of the town has a decidedly French appearance, with handsome villas surrounded by well-kept gardens, good roads with wide sidewalks, and shade trees to protect one from the sun; while in old Cairo everything is as unchanged as in Stamboul or Damascus.

On Thursday, February 19th, I drove to the ruins of Heliopolis, or "City of the Sun." The only object of interest there is the celebrated obelisk, similar to those now standing in Paris, Rome, London, and New York. In the neighbourhood is the sycamore tree under which the Holy Family are said to have rested during their flight into Egypt. The tree certainly does not look as if it were 1800 years old, and if that is a fact it is a miracle. A short distance from this tree is an ostrich farm, owned by a French company, where nearly a thousand of the birds are kept. It is well worth a visit, everything about the place being admirably arranged.

As I was driving back I met the new Khedive, who looks like an amiable and intelligent young prince. I also passed a large number of Egyptian troops, who are an exceptionally fine body of men. A great change has taken place in the efficiency of the army since it was reorganized under British officers. In Cairo one meets many of the Moslem ladies driving in broughams. They wear but a thin gossamer veil over their faces, so that their features can be seen easily. Many of them are very beautiful, with large, lustrous black eyes and fine complexions.

In the afternoon I visited the old Mosque of the Sultan Hassan, which dates from 1357, and which, though rather dilapidated, is con-

The Sphinx.

sidered by some judges the finest in Cairo. Then I went to the citadel, and saw the superb modern Mosque of Mehemet Ali, built in 1829, the interior of which is of Oriental alabaster. From the citadel a grand view is obtained of the city and surrounding country, the pyramids being plainly visible. The other objects of interest are the spot where the Mamelukes were slaughtered (all but one—Emin Bey, who jumped his horse down the terrace, killing the animal but sav-

Gate of the Citadel, Cairo.

ing his own life); and Joseph's Well, which is not called after him of the coat of many colours, but after Saladin, whose name in Arabic was Youssoof, or Joseph. Continuing to the tombs of the Caliphs, I lingered to see where the late Khedive was buried about a month before, and, after a short stop in the bazaar, got back to Shepheard's in time for a refreshing cup of afternoon tea on the hotel terrace facing the street, where all the guests congregate at this hour.

Friday, February 10th, I spent pleasantly, visiting old Cairo, where the curious Coptic church is built over a spot at which it is said the Virgin, St. Joseph, and the child Jesus Christ rested during the flight into Egypt. The church is very old and curious. The priests, I am sorry to say, I found as anxious for backsheesh as any Mohammedans. The Mosque of Omar, now deserted, is interesting; so also is the nilometer, which marks the rise of the Nile. After this I passed the tombs of the Mamelukes, and saw the dancing and howling dervishes; and I left Cairo in a sleeping-car, at 7 P. M., for Assiout.

Bedouins carrying their children.

CHAPTER XI.

ON THE NILE.

ATURDAY, February 20th, I arrived at Assiout at 6 A. M., going at once on board the steamboat Amerartas, of Thomas Cook and Son's Nile flotilla, and soon afterward set out on my way south. Assiout is two hundred and twenty-three miles from Cairo by train, and a little farther by the river. The water of the Nile is very muddy, and the spots on the shore that are irrigated are green and beautiful to look upon, but the land elsewhere is dreary and uninhabited. In many places it reminded me of the Colorado River at Fort Yuma, in Arizona Territory. The flies in Upper Egypt are a great nuisance, and one must have a brush always ready to keep them off.

At sunset we arrived at Girgeh, after a voyage of eighty-eight miles, and made fast to the bank for the night. This is mostly a modern town, the only object of interest being the Latin monastery, the oldest establishment of its kind in Egypt.

Throughout this country are many caves, which in the early days of Christianity were inhabited by pious monks and hermits, who thought they were pleasing God by mortifying the flesh, fasting, and living in dirt and filth, and who in the fulfilment of absurd vows went into the desert to live in a tomb or cavern to carry out self-inflicted penances. Let us be thankful that we live in an age when cleanliness and decency, as well as godliness, are considered requisites of a good Christian in a large part of the world, though not, I am sorry to say, where our religion originated. It is in Palestine and Egypt that a new reformation should occur, to purify the habits and ideas of the people, and to obliterate the spurious sacred places which so greatly encourage superstition among the ignorant.

On Sunday, February 21st, we were able to see a greater width of arable land, and we passed many villages of mud houses, surrounded by date-palms and filled with dirty Arabs. They were very picturesque, however, as seen from the deck of the steamboat.

Among our passengers was General Grenfell, the Sirdar or commander-in-chief of the Khedive's army, accompanied by his staff. He is a large, fine-looking man, amiable and entertaining. To him is due in a large measure the present efficiency of the Egyptian army, and the gradual reduction of taxation in the land. At night on the Nile the air in winter is keen and cold, and the passenger requires heavy clothing; but for several hours during the day the sun is hot, and the glare is trying to one's eyes, even when he takes the precaution to wear smoked-glass spectacles.

We moored for the night at Keneh, where were several *dahabeahs*, and also the tourist steamer that makes the voyage to the First Cataract, returning in three weeks. These prolonged trips I should think would be tedious, for there is such a sameness in the scenery that a half-hour's sail gives one a perfect idea of what the rest will be.

Soudanese warrior.

Monday, February 22d, we arrived at Luxor at 3.30 P. M.; but I decided to proceed to Assouan, and visit the ruins of Thebes, Karnak, and Luxor on my return. We left again at 4.30, and lay up for the night at Esneh. The crop raised here is mostly sugar-cane, and at different points on the river there are numerous refineries, some very large, with the most modern machinery.

A dahabiah on the Nile.

Tuesday, February 23d, at 10 A. M., we stopped at Edfou. Here is a fine temple, the inspection of which we reserved for the return trip, when the boat makes a longer tarry. On the bank were a group of about fifty wild-looking Soudanese or Nubians, the first we had seen. They have but little clothing, wear their hair in long ringlets, and are an active, muscular race, far more courageous than the patient, much-abused Egyptian fellaheen.

While we delayed at Edfou, Sir Francis Grenfell, in full uniform, gave a reception on the deck of the Amerartas to the officials and sheiks of that district. They were refreshed with coffee and cigarettes, and then left with much hand-kissing and salaaming. Going on shore, they performed a sort of war-dance, with a brandishment of their large, two-handed swords and spears, which ended the ceremony.

On the Nile trip we met many *dahabeahs* with parties of tourists and invalids. Only two flags were represented—the English and the American—those carrying the Stars and Stripes being in a majority of about three to one. At Daraou there was another reception, in which Sir Francis Grenfell was the personage welcomed. As we approached, a large Bedouin sheik, dressed in a long scarlet robe and snow-white turban, carrying a huge scimetar in a silver scabbard, and mounted on a beautiful chestnut Arabian stallion in purple caparisons embroidered with gold, awaited the arrival of the boat. He was accompanied by a retinue mounted on camels and horses, the whole forming an interesting assemblage.

As we were to lie at Daraou all night, I took advantage of the two hours of daylight remaining to go on donkey-back to the town, a half-mile distant. My road lay over a dusty plain, and I never have seen a more miserable village. Its houses are built of sun-dried mud bricks, presenting no evidences of comfort. Still, the people seemed to be cheerful and happy, showing that wealth and luxury are not indispensable for making men so.

That evening, after dinner, three lovely young English girls, who were in the party of General and Lady Grenfell, sang, with banjo accompaniment, such familiar airs as "Marching through Georgia," "Way down upon the Suwanee River," and "Rally round the Flag, Boys!" and the effect over the still waters of the Nile was delightful. It seems that the old American war-songs have just reached England, and at present are very popular there.

A Turkish and an Egyptian woman.

On Wednesday, February 24th, we arrived at Assouan, at 9 A. M. This town, seven hundred and fifty miles from the Mediterranean and five hundred and eighty-five miles from Cairo, is the market for the Soudan and Central Africa. The population, about four thousand, is composed of Arabs, Greeks, negroes, Soudanese, and Bedouins, in every style of dress and undress. The bazaar contains wild beasts' skins, ebony clubs, lances, poisoned arrows, and necklaces of beads and shells.

The Nubian girls are lithe, slight, and stately; and I was struck with the appropriateness to them of the description of Mother Eve, as being "in naked beauty more adorned," their sole costume in this serene and glowing climate being an apron around the loins—and somewhat of the slenderest too—composed of loose thongs of leather decorated with small shells.

There were five of us who soon after our arrival set out on donkeys. My companions were three young Frenchmen such as one rarely finds except on the Boulevards in Paris, or at Trouville or Dieppe, and a stolid German from Leipsic. None of these gentlemen could speak a word of any language except his own; so that the conversation, while friendly, was not animated. We galloped through the narrow streets of Assouan, and then struck out into the desert, passing a dreary Moslem cemetery, where a funeral was taking place. Men were lowering the body into the subterranean chamber that receives the Moslem dead, and at a little distance was a group of women loudly wailing and lamenting. Soon after this we reached the granite quarries where all the obelisks that have stood in Egypt were obtained. One still lies uncompleted in the quarry, rendered useless by a large flaw. Leaving the quarries, we went on through the barren, sandy plain, until we came to the river, nearly opposite the sacred isle of Philæ, and crossed in a large boat, rowed by eight lusty Nubians. Philæ is a small island which formerly was entirely covered with buildings. The principal ruins now remaining are the great Temple of Isis, founded by Ptolemy II, or

Philadelphus; the Temples of Æsculapius and Athor, the Egyptian Venus; and the so-called Pharaoh's bed. The Temple of Isis is almost whole; the carvings and colouring are well preserved, and the entire effect is impressive and beautiful. I am ashamed to be obliged to record the fact that the early Christians defaced with hammers and mud all the fine carving and painting that was accessible to them.

An excellent luncheon was sent up from the steamboat, and we picknicked in the temple.

Opposite Philæ is the starting-point for Wady Halfa and the Second Cataract, and the steamboat was now at the wharf; but my time would not permit me to go farther into the desert. We descended the cataract in our boat to Assouan, stopping at a dangerous point to see some naked Nubians ride logs through the boiling current. We took a different channel, and found running the rapids—for that is what we should call them in America—pleasant, exciting, and not at all dangerous. From Philæ to Assouan the scenery is wild and weird. Miss Martineau calls it, with much aptness, "fantastic and impish"—the large rocks having been cut into all kinds of peculiar shapes by the immemorial action of the water at the times of annual inundation. The colour, too, is often black and polished, with a gleam like that of anthracite coal. To add to the strangeness of the scene, the boatmen sang occasionally a sort of Gregorian chant, which echoed among the crags; and the sense of aged Egypt—the land where the same Sphinx that Œdipus questioned still stares over the "antres vast and deserts idle"—broods in everything, invincibly powerful.

By 4 P. M. we were landed at Assouan, and we spent the rest of the afternoon in the bazaar, bargaining with the natives, returning to the Amerartas in time for the eight-o'clock dinner. The evenings were always delightful, and I cannot tell what a feeling of contentment comes over the journeyer as he sits on deck after a good repast, sipping a cup of *café turque*, and perhaps listening to the strains of music that steal across the water from some neighbouring *dahabeah*. To get away from business and newspapers, and to divert the

Sphinx at Karnak.

thoughts into totally different channels, is a grand sanitation, which acts like a tonic on the mind and body and adds years to one's life. That night I slept well — whether from fatigue, or from the feeling of satisfaction and exultation at having penetrated into Nubia, I cannot now remember.

In Egypt is to be found the earliest authentic record of humanity, extending 5,004 years before the Christian era. The history has been divided into ten periods, viz.:

Ancient Egyptian Empire	B.C. 5004 to B.C. 3064.
Middle Egyptian Empire	B.C. 3064 to B.C. 1703.
New Egyptian Empire	B.C. 1703 to B.C. 525.
Persian domination	B.C. 525 to B.C. 323.
Ptolemaic period	B.C. 323 to B.C. 30.
Roman domination	B.C. 30 to A.D. 395.
Byzantine period	A.D. 395 to A.D. 638.
Arab period	A.D. 638 to A.D. 1517.
Turkish domination	A.D. 1517 to A.D. 1798.
Modern period	A.D. 1798 to A.D. 1893.

The ancient Egyptians have left on their monuments the imperishable traces of their habits, their customs, and their history; and those traces show a very civilized condition to have existed. In religion they at first believed in but one God; later, polytheism spread through the land, and each city had its own series of deities, but all worshipped the chief gods, Osiris and Isis. During the Roman domination Christianity supplanted the ancient worship; and afterward, in the Arab period, Mohammedanism almost entirely drove out Christianity. The Copts of the present day are the representatives of those who remained faithful to the Cross. By the last census they numbered four hundred thousand out of a population of six million eight hundred thousand.

Egypt has always been an agricultural country, owing to the splendid crops grown in the fertile belt of the Nile, where irrigation prevails, and where cheap labour makes possible competition with other countries. The chief articles of export are sugar and cotton; but the latter at present, by reason of the late enormous crops in America, pays but small profits.

On Thursday, February 25th, I crossed over to a spot directly opposite that where our steamboat lay. After climbing a steep, sandy hill, I entered the opening of the tombs that were discovered recently

A native of the Soudan.

by Sir Francis Grenfell and have been excavated by his order. The painted figures inside are almost as distinct and fresh as if made but yesterday. I then went to the island of Elephantine, which faces the town of Assouan. At one end of the island is a grove of palms, shading several pretty houses, which were covered with a purple flowering creeper. At the other end—the island being nearly a mile

A bride going to her husband. Egypt.

in length—is a vast quantity of the *débris* of half-demolished temples. These are of Saracenic origin, but no attempt has been made to study them. Fragments of statues, an altar, a gateway—all so ruined as to give little hint of their original form—alone remain of the architecture that once adorned the island. There were formerly two fine temples in a good state of preservation; but seventy years ago they were demolished because the Governor of Assouan wanted the stones for a palace. There is still a Roman quay, built of material taken from more ancient structures. The inhabitants of the island are mainly Nubians.

At 2 P. M. the Ameratas began her return voyage down the river, remaining all night again at Daraou, and arriving on Friday morning, February 26th, bright and early, at Edfou, where I took a donkey and rode about half a mile to the magnificent temple, the most perfect in all Egypt. A few years ago a modern village completely covered the temple itself up to the propylon, and rubbish filled the interior; but by order of the Khedive an entire excavation of the temple has been accomplished, under the direction of Mariette Bey. The temple is four hundred and fifty feet long, the propylon two hundred and fifty feet broad, and the towers one hundred and fifteen feet high, ascended by two hundred and fifty steps. The top commands a splendid view of the valley of the Nile, which at this point is broad and well irrigated.

This temple was begun by Ptolemy IV, Philopator, and continued by the succeeding sovereigns of the same family. It was dedicated to the worship of Hor-Hat and his mother Athor, the Egyptian Venus. In the inscription, Hor-Hat is called "Lord of the Heaven above, Son of Osiris, King of all Kings, of both Lower and Upper Egypt, and Master of all Gods and Goddesses." The completion of the temple required ninety-five years of actual work, which extended over a period of one hundred and seventy years. The great court, about one hundred and forty by one hundred and fifty feet, is surrounded on three sides by thirty-two dissimilar columns. The pronaos contains immense pillars covered with hieroglyphics, while in the adytum are twelve very peculiar columns, small at the base and bulging in the middle. There are numerous other smaller chambers leading up to the naos or sanctuary, in which the sacred hawk, the emblem of Hor-Hat, was deposited—a granite monolith made by Nectanebo I of the thirtieth dynasty, for an older temple built previously on the same spot. Here again, to some extent, the fine figures have been injured by over-zealous Christians of early times, who erroneously regarded the images as idols.

I had taken but a slight repast before starting, and on my return at 9 A. M. I found breakfast waiting, which it is needless to say I had abundant appetite to appreciate. Our steward, a fat little Greek, was an excellent *chef*, and, the disadvantages under which he laboured being considered, he did wonders, and was entitled to much credit.

While we lay at Edfou a group of Nubians collected on the shore, waiting in hopes of getting some backsheesh. To one pretty girl with beautiful white teeth, trim figure, and laughing black eyes —in fact, a perfect Venus *noire*—I gave a large slice of bread thickly covered with orange marmalade, and was much amused to see the result. The entire band collected round her, and she broke up the bread, putting a little marmalade on each piece, and giving every one a taste. The flavour was a new sensation to them, and they smacked their lips over it with evident delight.

At 1.30 we stopped as Esneh, thirty-five miles from Luxor, a place of considerable importance for those parts, having a population of seven thousand. It has been called "the most picturesque and amusing city of the upper Nile." A walk of about ten minutes from the boat-landing brought us to the portico of the great temple, the top being on a level with the town. Only the portico has been excavated, the work having been done in 1842, by order of Mehemet Ali. It is supposed that the remainder of the temple is under the neighbouring houses of the town. The portico contains

Tombs of the kings, Thebes.

twenty-four columns, each nineteen feet in circumference and sixty-five feet in height, the capitals being beautifully carved in designs of the palm, papyrus, and grapevine. The sculpture and hieroglyphics, although not considered so fine as in some of the earlier temples, are certainly very effective. If the remainder of the building when uncovered should prove to be on the same scale as the portico, it is grand indeed.

At 6.30 P. M. we moored at Luxor, and after dinner left the Amerartas for the Luxor Hotel—an agreeable change after a week on the steamboat. This hotel is in a large garden of palms, acacias, and flower-beds. Wandering around under the trees was an enormous pelican, quite tame and inoffensive.

On Saturday, February 27th, I committed myself, for a four days' sojourn at Luxor, to the charge of that necessary evil, a local guide, one Ahmed Abdullah; and with him I set out and crossed the Nile to the west side, where I found donkeys awaiting us. An hour's ride brought us to the Temple of Koorneh, where we made a short halt. This temple, dedicated to Amun, and built by Sethi I and Rameses II, was probably a fine work originally, but it is now much dilapidated. We left soon, and then after a tiresome ride of more than an hour, over the desert and through the dreary, desolate valley of Bab-el-Molook, we arrived at the Tomb of the Kings. Here were laid to rest the monarchs of the nineteenth and twentieth dynasties, and in an adjacent valley those of the eighteenth. These tombs are cut in the solid rock on the side-hill, and consist of long passages, within which are occasionally small rooms; and at the extreme end of a passage was once placed the sarcophagus. The body, carefully embalmed, and invested with all the surroundings of the exalted rank of the royal mummy, was with the sarcophagus put out of sight, as was supposed, forever, the entrance being walled up and covered with earth, so that soon all trace of the existence of the tomb was lost. Indeed, in some instances false chambers were arranged to mislead future explorers, while the real receptacle was carefully concealed. Twenty-five tombs in this valley have been opened thus far, and there are undoubtedly in the vicinity many more as yet unknown. Those considered the finest are, the tomb of Sethi I, called Belzoni's, that of Rameses III, or Bruce's Tomb, and that of Rameses IV.

The sculpture, painting, and hieroglyphics are wonderfully distinct. I had taken with me a quantity of magnesium wire, and by burning it in the dark places got an excellent view not otherwise obtainable. Belzoni's Tomb extends into the rock four hundred and seventy feet, it being the largest as well as the finest yet discovered. I returned by a different route from the one by which I came, climbing over the Libyan Mountain, from the top of which a splendid panorama of the surrounding country is presented. It is a hot, dusty, fatiguing walk, but worth the trouble, besides being the shortest road to the Temple of Dayr-el-Bahree, where I stopped for a few moments, and then finished the sight-seeing for the day at the Memnonium, or Ramaseum, which is a grand edifice and without a rival of its kind for beautiful architecture. In this temple was the largest statue ever carved in Egypt from a solid block. It is calculated to have weighed eight hundred and eighty-seven tons. By some means not now known this gigantic figure was thrown down and broken, and only a part of it remains.

On the way back to the river we passed the two colossi, both representing Amunoph. These were originally monoliths sixty feet high, with pedestals ten feet high, standing on the plain.

In Egypt the continuous sunshine is very trying to one's eyes, and I can understand henceforth the feelings of the Englishman who exclaimed, as he came up the Thames from Gravesend in a London fog, "Thank God, I am now in a country where the sun does not always shine!" For my own part, I consider the climate of the region between New York and Newport the finest in the world. It is neither too cold nor too warm, too wet nor too dry, and yet there is sufficient variety.

That evening I was invited by the German consular agent to an

The Great Temple at Karnak.

entertainment at his house, where the celebrated *danse du ventre* was performed admirably before an audience of ladies and gentlemen, all Germans but me. The dancers were five Arab girls, the music being executed by several native men.

Sunday, February 28th, in the *salon* of the hotel, we had morning service, with a sermon, conducted by the English chaplain, assisted by the Lord Bishop of Ontario. In the afternoon I saw Karnak, that enormous temple built during the nineteenth and twentieth dynasties. They must have been a stupendous sight in the days of Theban prosperity, those avenues of sphinxes, the great hall supported by hundreds of solid pillars, the magnificent obelisks and statues, the beautiful sculpture, the curious hieroglyphics, the massive gateways, and the cartouches of the various kings.

The temple, which is a mile from Luxor, is about a mile and three-quarters in circumference. The walls were eighty feet high and twenty-five feet thick at the base. There were four obelisks originally; now only two remain, one of which, that of Queen Hatasoo, is the largest ever made, being ninety-two feet high and eight feet square at the base. It was originally surmounted by a small pyramid of pure gold, and the whole, from top to bottom, was gilded. I could not help thinking what a marvellous race of people these ancient Egyptians were, to have left behind them such lasting monuments of their wealth and greatness. We of this generation have thus far produced nothing that will endure for three thousand years.

On Monday, February 29th, I again crossed the river and this time wended my way to the splendid remains of the Temple of Medeenet-Haboo. It is really two temples, that of Thothmes III and that of Rameses III. The north base is especially rich in hieroglyphics, containing ten historical representations of Egyptian victories—one of them the only known Egyptian picture of a naval fight. In the centre of the great court of the temple are the remains of the Coptic cathedral, which fortunately has been totally demolished, so one can discern perfectly the majestic proportions of the great edifice.

Near all the ruins are numerous venders of curiosities, of which some are real and some spurious, but so cleverly made that they defy detection even by an expert.

Tuesday, March 1st, I spent in examining the Luxor Temple. It is quite near the hotel, and I had therefore left it for the last. This building was constructed under the eighteenth dynasty, during the reign of Amunoph III, about 1600 B. C. The colonnade was added under Horis, and the two obelisks and the huge statues and the pylon were placed there by Rameses II. Of the two obelisks that formerly graced this temple, one is now erected in the Place de la Concorde, Paris, the other being left in solitary grandeur on its original site.

After dinner that evening I finished my visit to Luxor, and slept on board the steamboat Nefert-Ari, leaving for the return trip at daylight on the morning of Wednesday, March 2d. At breakfast-time we found ourselves at Kench, and soon afterward we left the Nefert-Ari in a rowboat, crossed the river, and went on donkeys to the Temple of Denderah, about an hour's ride. This edifice was begun by Ptolemy XII and completed by Tiberius, much of the ornamentation having been made during the reign of Nero. Its age, approximately, is eighteen hundred and fifty years. Mingled with its Egyptian style is an influence of Greek and Roman architecture. It was dedicated to Athor. It was one of the best preserved of all the temples on the Nile, and to me the most satisfactory, with perhaps the exception of the one at Edfou.

At 11.30 we resumed our trip down the Nile. I witnessed an interesting sight at Dechna, a little village directly on the bank, where we stopped at 2 P. M. Several thousand men and women—the latter standing in a group by themselves—were assembled, and as the steamboat approached they set up a dismal howl, which they sustained until we got out of hearing. It transpired that on our boat were twenty-five conscripts for the army, on their way to Cairo, and the unhappy people on the bank were the friends and relatives lamenting their loss, for the term of service of the Egyptian soldier is practically for

Obelisks, Karnak.

life. The poor conscripts were huddled together, squatting on the deck, under a guard of armed soldiers, and were not permitted to answer the salutations and farewells.

I was sorry to miss seeing the Coptic monastery of Sitteh Mariam-el-Adra (Lady Mary the Virgin), usually known as the Monastery of the Pulley. This is below Assiout, where I left the steamboat, and it is on a high precipice. The monastery is walled in for protection, and there is a cleft in the rocks down to the river. Formerly, as *dahabeahs* and steamboats were seen approaching, the pious monks would rush down, strip off their clothes, leap into the river, and swim out to demand backsheesh. Of late years this proceeding has been stopped by order of their patriarch, who came to the conclusion that it was not perfectly dignified.

Via Dolorosa, Jerusalem.

CHAPTER XII.

VISIT TO PALESTINE.

HURSDAY, March 3d, at 3 P. M., we were once more at Assiout. This city is the capital of Upper Egypt. It has a population of twenty-five thousand, and enjoys a considerable trade in various commodities. The mountains back of the town are covered with ancient tombs, where lived a large number of Christian anchorites at one period, and some noted saints have spent their lives at this spot in continuous fasting and prayer.

Curzon, in his "Visits to the Monasteries of the Levant," relates an incident of St. Macarius, who spent sixty years as a hermit in various places in the Egyptian desert, and was considered a model recluse. "Having thoughtlessly killed a gnat which was biting him, he was so unhappy at what he had done that, to make amends for his inadvertence,

Colossal statues of Memnon, Thebes.

and to increase his mortification, he retired to the marshes of Scete, where there were flies whose powerful stings were sufficient to pierce the hide of a wild boar; here he remained six months, till his body was so much disfigured that on his return his brethren only knew him by the sound of his voice." These anchorites were somewhat like the Hindu fakirs that one sees at the present day in the holy places in India, and they must have been, as the fakirs are, disgusting objects.

At 9 P.M. I left Assiout in a sleeping-car, getting back to Cairo at 8 A.M. the next morning, and I felt inclined to sing that old negro melody, "Ain't I glad to get out of the wilderness!" The dust and flies, together with the incessant wrangling of the donkey-boys, porters, and guides, and the never-ceasing demand for backsheesh, tire one's patience. The Arabs are a nation of thieves, and have no conscience whatever. I caught one donkey-boy with his hand in my coat pocket, in which I had a few piasters; and on the sleeping-car a German gentleman found that his valise had been abstracted and taken to the toilet-room, where it was cut open and the most valuable articles carried away, the remainder, which the thief could not take, being thrown into the water-closet. On

An Egyptian Woman

the train was a detective, a dirty Arab, who took the matter very coolly, displayed no interest in the theft, and said the act was one that occurred there frequently.

Friday, March 4th, I again took up my quarters at Shepheard's Hotel, remaining until the following Wednesday. Those five days were spent pleasantly with friends whom I found there, among them my cousin, Count Gabriel Diodati. There were also plenty of letters to read and answer, together with excursions to Sakkara and Memphis, to see the statues of Rameses II, the pyramids, and the wonderful subterranean tombs of the sacred bulls. Then there were driving, donkey-riding, visiting the bazaar, etc. The terrace at Shepheard's Hotel, of an afternoon when the band of an English regiment plays, is one of the most amusing places that I know of. Groups of guests, mostly English and Americans, sit taking their tea, while in the street below are passing a throng of picturesquely dressed people of all nationalities and creeds—Turks, Arabs, with occasionally a green-turbaned descendant of

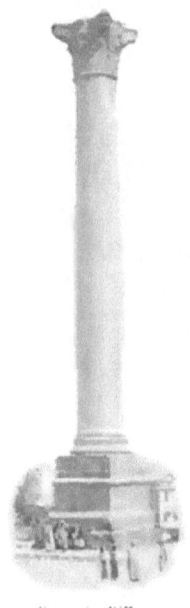

Pompey's Pillar,
Alexandria.

the Prophet, Greek priests in their curious black robes and queer-shaped hats, and now and then a carriage graced with harem ladies whose beauty is rather enhanced by the thin white veils that are supposed to hide their features. Before their carriages are usually two runners with long sticks to clear the way, and on the box sits a tall, coal-black eunuch, to guard them from all harm. Then pass some lobster-coated English foot soldiers, or two or three officers on horseback, with their little pillbox hats set on "three hairs." Perhaps an Egyptian regiment with music then goes by, or the young Khedive on his way to the palace. It is a curious and interesting sight, this mingling of European "high-lifers" and devout adherents of the Koran.

On Wednesday, March 6th, at 9.30 A. M., I left Cairo in the train, arriving at Alexandria at 1 P. M. This railway is fairly well built, and the trains run at about the average speed of a local American line. We passed through the rich, arable land of the Delta, where enormous crops are raised. I went to the Khedevial Hotel, where I had breakfast, after which, in company with a guide, I drove to Pompey's Pillar, along the Mahmoudeah Canal, where there are many fine villas, to the Catacombs, to the palace, and to the so-called tomb of Cleopatra.

Modern Alexandria is a thoroughly French city. The streets

A Mohammedan sheik.

which are wide, are paved with blocks of stone two or three feet long, and are kept clean and in good order. In the evening one sees many fine turnouts, all in European style. That night, with a friend who had been my fellow-passenger across the Pacific Ocean, and under the guidance of a cicerone, I saw some of the famous dancers for whom Alexandria is noted. Their performance is similar to that which we witnessed at Luxor.

By ten o'clock of Thursday, March 10th, I found myself on board the Khedevial Line steamer Mahallah, eight hundred tons, and soon it was *Partant pour la Syrie*. In the first cabin every available place was taken, mostly by Americans bound for the Holy Land. The steerage was filled with the most motley assemblage I had yet encountered — Russian Jews, dancing dervishes, Copts, Italians, Greeks, and Mohammedans. Most of them spent much of their time in praying, especially the Jews, who no doubt were greatly excited at approaching the land of their forefathers. The sea at first was rough, and almost immediately after leaving the breakwater at Alexandria every one was violently seasick; but in a short time we ran into smooth water, and the passengers began to revive. The rest of the voyage was delightful.

On Friday the sea continued quiet, and we arrived off Jaffa at 12.30, and debarked without difficulty. Although the sea was said to be unusually smooth, there was nevertheless considerable rolling, and several ladies were made seasick by the motion of the small boat. We were rowed ashore in one of Thomas Cook and Son's boats, for here as well as in Egypt they have all control of the ways, and one must travel with their tickets.

After landing we had a long walk to take, up many steps and through a market-place filled with a noisy crowd of natives. Then we were conveyed in carriages to the Hotel Jerusalem, kept by a German, who provided us with luncheon; and then I set out for Ramleh by carriage and three horses, with a Roman Catholic dragoman named Tanoos. We went for some distance through the town of Jaffa or Yâfa, the Joppa so frequently mentioned in Holy Writ

Here St. Peter the apostle raised Dorcas to life, and beheld the vision showing him that the difference between the Hebrews and the Gentiles was to cease. For a thousand years Jaffa has been the landing-place of pilgrims who visit the sacred shrines of Jerusalem. The house of Simon the tanner is shown, but of course is of doubtful authenticity. There are several monasteries in Jaffa, and also Miss Arnott's school, which is doing an excellent work among the girls of the city. Just outside the gates is the German colony, which came in and took possession of the site originally occupied by an unsuccessful American colony.

Leaving Jaffa, we passed through many orange groves, and then entered the plains of Sharon, which were green and fertile, with many wild flowers along the roadside. Here grew the rose of Sharon, which is supposed to have been a species of mallow. In three hours I had arrived in Ramleh, and after securing a room at Reinhart's Hotel I mounted the stairs of the Great Tower, near the hotel, and had a splendid view of the country for many miles in all directions. I was surprised and delighted with the beauty and apparent fertility of this part of Palestine. The land may be to some extent worn out, but by proper cultivation and the use of fertilizers it could be made very productive.

On Saturday I was impatient to continue my journey; so by eight o'clock I got away from Ramleh and proceeded toward Jerusalem. A French company is building a line of railway here, but the work is going on slowly, and it will be some time before it is completed. After about an hour we reached a hill, and thence spread out before us lay the valley of Ajalon, where Joshua defeated the five kings of the Amorites, and where he commanded the sun and the moon to stand still until he had completely destroyed his enemies: "Sun, stand thou still upon Gibeon—and thou, Moon, in the valley of Ajalon." A little farther on we passed the village of Latrûn, where, according to tradition, had resided the two thieves who were crucified with Christ. The country now became very sterile and

The Garden of Gethsemane.

rocky, and our route was a steep ascent. We passed Kolonieh, and in less than two hours more, at 3 P. M., we were within the walls of the sacred city.

I went to the Grand New Hotel, where I was fortunate in getting a room, it being crowded. Afterward, in company with the dragoman Tanoos, I went to the Church of the Holy Sepulchre and

The Damascus Gate, Jerusalem.

to the wailing-place of the Jews. The scene at the latter spot was curious. The women were crying, and kissing the stones of the temple, and the men were reading the Psalms or the Talmud. The Jews who live in Jerusalem now are all immigrants, or the descendants of immigrants to their own home, from other countries, mostly Russians, Poles, Germans, Spaniards, and Portuguese.

In the Church of the Holy Sepulchre the scene was to me very sad. I saw the Stone of Unction, the Station of Mary, the Sepulchre, the stone which the angel rolled away from our Lord's grave, the Column of the Scourging, Calvary, the rent in the rock, and the other spots considered sacred by a vast number of ignorant people. How discouraging it is to think that such imposture should be tolerated in the nineteenth century! Here is found the worst form of idolatry and imposition; and it would be well if the church and its contents could be obliterated by an earthquake, and a new and clean Christianity built up, worthy of our meek and lowly Saviour. If some rich philanthropist wishes to do a good work, he should establish a library and reading-room, and plenty of hot-water baths, free to the various orders of priests and monks in Jerusalem, and should encourage them to clean their bodies and elevate their minds.

The disgraceful fights between the Greeks, Latins, Armenians, and Copts are not so frequent as formerly, for the influx of European and American visitors is without doubt something of a restraint on them in many ways.

On Sunday I felt in duty bound to attend church in Jerusalem, and therefore went to early service at Christ's English Church. It was a great satisfaction to find that in one place within the walls of Mount Zion the pure gospel of Jesus was preached without any mummery, in a neat edifice, simple and appropriate, and the service rendered in a decorous manner.

Afterward, with the dragoman, I went over the Via Dolorosa, stopping at the stations of the Cross; to the Convent of the French Sisters of Zion; St. Stephen's Gate; the Garden of Gethsemane; the valley of Jehoshaphat; the Pool of Bethesda, which is now dry; the tomb of the Virgin; St. Veronica's House; the Church of St. Anne; and the Hospital of the Knights of St. John, otherwise the Knights of Malta. I then made a longer and more thorough visit to the Church of the Holy Sepulchre, and came away with the same feeling as before, of sadness and humiliation. When one visits the

The stone of unction, Jerusalem.

temples of the heathen one has a contempt for the humbug with which those poor people are duped; but to find this foolish superstition at the fountain-head of our own true religion makes one feel heartsick and despondent.

The Holy Sepulchre is in a small chapel in the centre of the rotunda of the church, and is built of marble. It is divided into two apartments. In the first is the stone that the angel rolled away from the tomb, and in the second is a marble slab said to cover the sepulchre of our Lord. This stone is cracked in the middle, and worn smooth by the kisses of many thousands of pilgrims. At one end of the apartment is a hole, from which on Easter Sunday the Greek Patriarch hands out the fire which he pretends has come down from heaven to light the candles on the altar. What a terrible account these patriarchs will have to settle with their Maker in the day of judgment for this imposition!

After luncheon I again set out with Tanoos and made a circuit of one part of the town. I had from the American consulate a *kawass* armed with a formidable scimitar, and also a soldier from the garrison. These are requisites to an entrance to the Mohammedan holy places. We went to the Mosque of Omar, which is on the site of Solomon's Temple upon the summit of Mount Moriah. A slab in the middle of the floor covers the Well of Departed Spirits, through which, according to Mohammedan tradition, all souls descend, and whence they will be brought up at the judgment day. There were many other remarkable sights, the most curious being the stone with three and a half nails sticking in it. There were nineteen, but Satan has knocked the others into the stone. When the remaining ones disappear the world will come to an end. Near by are the Mosque el-Aksa, inside of which is the beautiful pulpit of carved wood, the stone with the footprint of Christ, and the Well of the Leaf, which is one of the gates of paradise.

I descended an adjoining flight of steps to the Cradle of Christ, in which the infant Jesus is said to have been circumcised, and below which are the wonderful underground Stables of Solomon, the latter a remarkably interesting spot.

The interior of the Mosque of Omar is very handsome, the dome being especially beautiful. The traditions that centre upon this spot are wonderfully numerous. Here Ornan had his thrashing-floor; here Abraham built the altar on which he was about to sacrifice his son Isaac; and here stood Solomon's Temple. The mosque is octagonal,

Mosque of Omar, and Tribunal of David

each side being sixty-eight feet long, and is covered with coloured tiles. The date of its erection is uncertain, but there is little doubt that it is at least a thousand years old. The interior is divided by concentric circles of pillars and piers, the innermost of which support the great wooden dome, which is ninety-eight feet high and sixty-six feet in diameter. The inner walls, like the outer, are covered with tiles and inscribed with passages from the Koran. The Sacred Rock,

Interior of the tomb of the Virgin, Jerusalem.

under the dome, is a mass of rough stone that rises three or four feet above the marble floor, and is about sixty feet long. Under it is a cave. All manner of traditions attach to this rock. The chief Mussulman story is, that when Mohammed ascended to heaven from this place the rock wanted to follow, and actually rose six or seven feet (hence the cave); but the angel Gabriel stopped it at that point, and the prints of his fingers are still visible on the stone. Here the rock remained suspended. Your inquiry why there are side walls to the cave, apparently supporting the rock, is answered by the information that they are not necessary, but were merely built for the assurance and comfort of tourists, who were afraid to enter the cave when there was no visible support for its ponderous roof. Fergusson, the antiquary, believes that this is the tomb wherein the body of Christ was laid after the crucifixion.

I had a fine view of the valley of Jehoshaphat; the tombs of Absalom, Jacob, and Zachariah; the field that was bought with the thirty pieces of silver Judas received for betraying our Lord; the tree on which he hanged himself; the leper hospital; the tomb of David; and the Coenaculum, or Chamber of the Last Supper.

Again I went to the Jews' wailing-place, and before returning to the hotel saw the Armenian monastery, and the tomb of St. James on the spot where he was beheaded.

I spent a most interesting day, for, while the ground is heaped with what is spurious and fraudulent, yet the various landmarks are well authenticated.

It was a cool, clear morning on Monday, March 14th, when with Tanoos I set off on horseback for Jericho. We passed out of the Jaffa gate and made the tour of the city walls, taking then the road between the Garden of Gethsemane and the Virgin's tomb into the valley of Jehoshaphat, and thence up the Mount of Olives. The view of Jerusalem, surrounded by its high, castellated, mediæval wall, from this point is very picturesque and beautiful.

Soon after this, at Bethany, with his gun slung over his shoulder, came up the representative of the sheik who was sent to guard us, for even now it is dangerous to go to Jericho unprotected, as one may still "fall among thieves."

After four hours' progress we stopped at a khan, or stone inclosure for the protection of travellers, where we rested and had luncheon. This

Tomb of the Virgin, and Grotto of the Pater.

is said to be the spot of the parable of the good Samaritan who befriended the man "going down from Jerusalem to Jericho." A carriage road, expected to reach completion in a year, was in process of construction. The road lay through a rugged, mountainous country of but little vegetation, and the temperature became perceptibly higher as we neared our destination. On the descent of the hill into the valley a grand scene was spread out before us. On one side was the mountain where our Lord was tempted of the devil, and in front the river Jordan and the Dead Sea, while away in the distance stood Mounts Pisgah, Nebo, and Hermon.

The rock in the Mosque of Omar.

The Jericho of Joshua's triumph is not the same as the modern village of the same name. Some round mounds are all that is left of the ancient city. Bible scholars know well the story of Jericho's siege and capture, of the spies that were entertained by Rahab the harlot, of the children of Israel marching round the city, and of the blasts of the trumpet each day, until, on the seventh, the walls fell down and God's chosen people rushed in and destroyed their enemies.

It was from Jericho that the prophet Elijah went forth with Elisha and witnessed the translation of the latter in a chariot of fire, carried by a whirlwind up to heaven.

I arrived at the Jordan Hotel at Jericho at 4 P. M., and the proprietor at once brought me a cup of refreshing tea. I was well content to rest for the remainder of the day, preparatory to a hard day's work on the morrow. At dinner I had an interesting talk, through an interpreter, with the Turkish military commander at Jerusalem, who had come up to inquire into the plague of locusts which was devastating this part of Palestine. He told me that he was one of forty-eight children, and that his father was a man of great importance in Turkistan.

On Tuesday we were off for the Dead Sea by 7 A. M., and reached its shore in two hours. Our way lay through an arid plain, hot and dusty, with here and there a little vegetation. I was surprised to find that the water of the Dead Sea was clear and sparkling, and that it washed a gravelly shore. The scenery is desolate and weird. On either side the mountains rise abruptly, barren and harsh, without trees or grass.

The Dead Sea is forty-six miles long, and nine and a half miles wide in the widest place. This is the measurement made by Lieutenant Lynch, in the month of April. The lake varies somewhat with the rainfall of different seasons. Into the Dead Sea flows the river Jordan, this fresh though muddy stream being lost in the bitter salt waters. Numerous events of biblical record happened on these Dead Sea shores. It was here that Lot's wife, for looking back in disobedience to the command of the Lord, was turned into a pillar of salt.

I undressed and went into the water for a bath, and found it very pleasant, as I did not mind the stinging sensation to the skin. In my attempts to swim, my feet went into the air, the water being so buoyant, and it was difficult to make any headway. The bath there I found much more agreeable than in the Jordan, where there is a strong current of dirty water, and a muddy and sticky bank, which makes it not only very disagreeable but also somewhat dangerous to bathe there. When we were leaving the Dead Sea I was much interested by the performance of two Bedouin sheiks. They had a sham battle with their drawn scimitars, circling round each other on horseback, until one gave his antagonist the *coup de grâce* by pretending to cut his head off while both were at full gallop.

In an hour I arrived on the banks of the Jordan, and I must confess that I was much disappointed. The river is one hundred and twenty miles long, measured by a straight line from its source, through the Sea of Galilee to the Dead Sea; but it is in reality much longer on account of its vermicular windings. It is from five to twelve feet deep, and from eighty to one hundred and seventy feet wide. It was in the valley of the Jordan that John the Baptist preached the coming of the Messiah, and in the sacred waters of this river our Lord was baptized. At certain feasts of the Church thousands come from all quarters of the globe to wash away their sins in this stream sanctified by their Saviour. I saw many when I myself bathed there.

We had our luncheon at the Pilgrim Bathing Place, where it is supposed that John the Baptist baptized our Lord Jesus Christ. "And lo, the heavens were opened unto him, and he saw the Spirit of God descending like a dove, and lighting upon him: and lo a voice from heaven, saying, This is my beloved Son, in whom I am well pleased" (Matt. iii, 13–17). If this is not the exact spot, it is without doubt very close to it. Near it also is the place where the children of Israel crossed the Jordan dry shod and entered the promised land.

Tamoos, the dragoman, in telling me of the vast numbers of pilgrims

A scene on the river Jordan.

who come here at certain seasons to bathe together, said that he had
seen as many as five thousand on the banks of the river at one time.
We met several small parties of these pilgrims, poor fanatics, some
in waggons, some on donkeys, and others walking, dusty and footsore,
with their palmers' staves in their hands. Most of them looked as if

it were many weeks since their bodies had been refreshed by bathing
an abstinence that should have made them appreciate the cooling waters
of the Jordan, even if it was yellow with mud.

Returning again over the dry valley at half past two, I reached the
hotel, where our landlord, having been on the lookout for our approach,
had ready for me one of the excellent cups of tea for which he is famous.
The remainder of the day I spent quietly, with the exception of a walk to
the site of old Jericho, the city of Joshua's time. Rising directly over

this place is the Quarantania, or Temptation Mountain of the text: "And the devil, taking him up into a high mountain, showed unto him all the kingdoms of the world in a moment of time." On this side of the mountain are numerous caves in the rock, some of which are still inhabited by Greek monks.

On Wednesday, while the moon was still shining, I began the return trip from Jericho, reaching the Apostle's Well at 11 A. M., where we had luncheon. While we were there the Governor of Jerusalem passed by with a guard of soldiers. He is said to be unfriendly to Christians, but he bowed most politely to me. We went over the Mount of Olives; to the traditional house of Mary and Martha; to the tomb of Lazarus; to Paternoster Chapel; and to the spot shown as the place of the ascension of our Lord. The declivity of the Mount of Olives is steep and precipitous to the Garden of Gethsemane. Here I dismounted and went in. The garden is in charge of the Latin monks, who raise flowers which they present to visitors—expecting a few francs, however, as backsheesh. The olive trees are said to be the same that were there during the lifetime of our Lord, and they certainly look very old. Afterward I crossed over the road to the tombs of the Blessed Virgin, St. Anne, St. Joachim, and St. Joseph, and then rode into Jerusalem. Around Gethsemane was a crowd of loathsome lepers crying for alms, which was exceedingly disagreeable.

That afternoon I revisited the Church of the Holy Sepulchre, and attended service at the Armenian Convent, where the patriarch preached. The Armenians follow the Mohammedan fashion of leaving their shoes outside their place of worship and wearing their Fez caps or their turbans within it. The church is dedicated to St. James, and marks the spot where he was buried. One of the monks, high in authority, politely showed me his own room, where he had a library of the early fathers and many bottles of fine wine.

I then obtained from the head of the Franciscan Monastery (Roman Catholic) a certificate, written in Latin, to the effect that I had visited all the holy places, and was entitled to all the dispensa-

The Mount of Olives.

tions and privileges accruing therefrom, which are said to be very important.

On Thursday, in a carriage with three horses, I set out at 6 A. M. for Bethlehem, about one hour's drive from the Jaffa gate. The road thither is good, well constructed through a rocky country. The crops raised are principally olives, figs, and grapes. *En route* we passed quite close to the tree where Judas hanged himself after bestowing the fatal kiss on his Master, and to the tomb of Rachel.

Church of the Nativity, at Bethlehem.

Bethlehem is inhabited by native Christians, whose blood is said to have a large mixture of that of the Crusaders. Our way lay through a street that was only wide enough for one carriage to pass at a time, to the Church of the Nativity, where I alighted. The entrance is very small, and one can not pass through it upright.

Many persons who have examined into the subject think there is a strong probability that this place is the real site of the birth of Christ. It was generally considered to be so during the time of Justin Martyr, about one hundred years after the event took place, and St. Jerome, one of the greatest of the early fathers, was a firm believer in its authenticity, and spent thirty years in a cell adjoining the spot, studying, praying, and fasting.

A silver star with a hole in the centre, so that pious pilgrims may kiss the rock, indicates the place where our Lord was born. Above this are sixteen lamps, which are always kept burning. There are several other altars in the church, marking the place of the wooden manger (now in Rome); the altar of the Magi; and the Chapel of St. Joseph, on the spot whither the husband of the Blessed Virgin retired while the accouchement took place, and where an angel appeared to him commanding the flight into Egypt. Finally, there are the altar over the tomb of the twenty thousand victims of King Herod's cruel massacre of the innocents, and the tomb of Eusebius.

Adjoining the Church of the Nativity are the Latin Church of St. Catherine and the Franciscan and the Armenian monasteries; and at a short distance south is the Milk Grotto. The tradition concerning this is, that a drop of the Virgin's milk fell on the rock, turning the whole of it white; and that a visit there will increase in a miraculous manner the flow of milk in women who have but a scanty supply. Those who can not go to the grotto may derive the same benefit by eating the little cakes, containing some of the powdered rock, which are sold there by an old woman.

Outside the town of Bethlehem, perhaps a walk of half an hour, is the Shepherds' Field, where the shepherds were watching their flocks by night when the angel of the Lord appeared to them, as the text reads: " And there were in the same country shepherds abiding in the field, keeping watch over their flock by night. And, lo, the angel of the Lord came upon them, and the glory of the Lord shone

round about them; and they were sore afraid. And the angel said unto them, Fear not: for, behold, I bring you good tidings of great joy, which shall be to all people. For unto you is born this day in the city of David a Saviour, which is Christ the Lord. And this shall be a sign unto you: Ye shall find the babe wrapped in swaddling clothes, lying in a manger. And suddenly there was with the angel

Grotto of the Nativity, at Bethlehem.

a multitude of the heavenly host praising God, and saying, Glory to God in the highest, and on earth peace, good will toward men." In this field is a cave, which is fitted up as a Greek chapel.

One thing that strikes travellers as odd is the guard of Turkish soldiers in the Church of the Holy Sepulchre and the Church of the Nativity. This is a necessary precaution, however, for the priests and monks of different denominations frequently come into collision, and were it not for the presence of the guard affrays would undoubtedly occur oftener. Ten months before my visit, four persons were killed in the Church of the Nativity in a fight between Greeks and Latins. By eleven o'clock I was in Jerusalem again, and after looking at the Jewish synagogues and the tombs of the kings, I drove back to Jaffa.

On Friday, as I was not to sail until afternoon, I had a good opportunity to rest, of which I took advantage. During the morning I wandered about the town, and visited the house of Simon the tanner, from the flat roof of which a fine view of the Mediterranean is to be had.

Jew's Woman in palace tume.

It was somewhere near Jaffa that Jonah was cast into the sea and swallowed by the great fish, in whose belly he remained three days. Here also was laid the scene of the mythological story of Andromeda chained to a rock by the monster whom Perseus slew. I was interested to see on the shore many scallop-shells, for from them the Crusaders adopted that emblem for their coat of arms, the device being borne to the present day by the descendants of the mediaeval knights.

The present ruler of Turkey, Abdul-Hamid II, is without doubt the ablest Padishah that has reigned in the Ottoman Empire for many years; he is the ruler in fact as well as in name, and understands thoroughly every detail of the government of his country. The Sultan is extremely simple in his habits and manners, and despatches the business of the realm with great rapidity, but never before every particular has been thought over and is well understood by him. He always rises early, and he devotes almost the whole day to his duties as a sovereign, the monotony being broken perhaps by an audience to some foreign ambassador or distinguished stranger. In a remarkable degree he possesses the love of all around him, but every one feels instinctively his wonderful ability and his penetrating mind. The Sultan is

View of Jaffa from the house of Simon the Tanner.

a man of serious disposition, caring nothing for frivolity or pleasure, and it would be an unfortunate day for Moslem and Christian alike if any harm should befall Abdul-Hamid. Toward Americans and their country his course has been one of consistent friendship and kindness, and every returning minister of the United States has gone home enthusiastic over the cordiality and good will of the Sultan.

In mechanical and scientific appliances and discoveries he has always evinced the greatest curiosity, and from its inception he has taken a deep interest in the World's Fair at Chicago. A few remarkable facts in connection with the present reign may be summarized, as follows: Turkish finances have vastly improved, and no foreign loan has been contracted for the past sixteen years. Not only have roads been opened, but various railways have been built, which needs must improve the condition of commerce. Schools have increased considerably in number, and public instruction has never been so general as under the present ruler of Turkey. The army is in better condition than ever before. The world knows what a Turkish soldier is, but, notwithstanding his efficiency, the Sultan is pacifically inclined, believing that progress and happiness for the people can only be acquired through peace. He is certainly a great sovereign.

Paul's wall, Damascus.

CHAPTER XIII.

HOME THROUGH EUROPE.

T six P. M. I was conveyed on board the Khedivial Line steamer Rahmanieh, which, although small, was a comfortable and good boat, much superior to the Mahallah. The sea was calm, and the transfer of the passengers was accomplished without difficulty. The boatmen of Thomas Cook and Son are wonderfully skilful in boat management, conveying the passengers to and from the vessel in a remarkable way. We soon set sail, and had a pleasant voyage.

Our ship reached Beyrout on Saturday, at 9 A. M., in a heavy shower, but before we landed it had ceased. The harbour is very beautiful. Rising in the distance are the Lebanon mountains, the tops of which were then covered with snow. Beyrout is a modern town in appearance, and much superior to the ordinary Turkish cities. This fact is the result of the American mission schools, which have

Interior of a Jewish house at Damascus.

done an excellent work for many years in educating and civilizing the people. At present the English, French, and other European nations have also educational establishments there.

About half past ten I set out in a carriage for Baalbek, accompanied by a dragoman named Sabir, a Maronite Christian. Crossing the mountains, we encountered a snow flurry, and the snow lay in drifts on the mountain-side. I felt the cold very much, not having prepared for it. We had dinner at Chtaura, and afterward continued

Boat and caravan at Jaffa

our journey, arriving at Baalbek at 11 P. M. The wine at Chtaura is of excellent repute; some prefer it to that produced in the Medoc districts. The scenery along our route was grand, and the road was fine—as good as any in Europe. The landlord of the hotel at Baalbek was expecting me, and had a comfortable room ready.

On Sunday, March 20th, I got up early, and by half past six was out looking at the wonderful ruins of Baalbek. The temples here date from a very early time. "Baal" was the name given by the

Phœnicians and Canaanites to the sun, their chief deity. The Greeks called the place Heliopolis, but devoted the temple to the worship of Jupiter. The remains show that before its ruin this pile must have been indescribably magnificent. The wonder is, how its huge stones were ever placed in their proper position. The carving of the Corin-

View of Beyrut.

thian columns is exquisitely done, and the architecture throughout is very beautiful. In the western wall are three stones which are perhaps the biggest ever set in any building. The enormous blocks measure over sixty-three feet in length, thirteen feet in height, and thirteen feet in thickness. The ruins themselves are sublime.

At eight o'clock I returned to Chtaura, arriving there at twelve, and had luncheon. On the way we passed the so-called tomb of Noah.

Mohammedans at prayer in the Great Mosque at Damascus.

Soon after 1 P. M. I set out again for Damascus. Much of the scenery was fine, especially the stony mountain pass called the Wady-el-Karn, which in former years was infested with robbers, and it is an ideal place for them. After this, Sabir, the dragoman, pointed out to me the white dome of the mosque in the distance which marks the spot where Cain killed his brother Abel, and also the tomb of the latter; but it is of rather doubtful authenticity, one would say. Soon after this we entered Damascus, and I was much struck with the fine gardens and villas along the road, which are kept green and beautiful by means of irrigation. Damascus

Maronite priest of Mount Lebanon.

A girl of Nazareth.

is believed to be one of the oldest existing cities. It has outlived Tyre and Sidon, Palmyra, Baalbek, Nineveh, Babylon, Thebes, and Memphis, and is a flourishing city today.

We drove to the Victoria Hotel, where the landlord received me with great politeness and provided me with a pleasant room.

Monday I spent in viewing the objects of interest in Damascus: the Great Mosque, a fine building, which was formerly a Christian church, and is said to contain the head of John the Baptist; the Minaret of Jesus, named from the legend that this is the spot where our Saviour will alight when he comes to judge the world; the citadel; "the street called Straight," which runs through the

Christian quarter, where so many innocent people were ruthlessly massacred in 1860 by the fanatical Moslems; the Jews' quarter, where

Interior of the House of Shamadansch, Damascus.

I viewed the interior of the house of Stromboli and other rich Hebrews; the tomb of Saladin; the Gate of Bab-Kisân, where tradition says St. Paul was let down in a basket; the tomb of St. George; the Moslem cemetery, where two of Mohammed's wives and his daughter Fatima are buried; the houses of Ananias and Naaman the leper; and the wonderful bazaars. These bazaars are much more remarkable than those of Constantinople or Cairo, caravans coming hither from Bagdad, Teheran, and Mecca, bringing all kinds of rich merchandise, just as they did a thousand years ago.

Overlooking the city is Mount Hermon, and countless canals, drawn from the Barada, furnish numerous fountains for the use of the inhabitants. By the Arabs Damascus is considered the earthly paradise, and they call one of the city gates God's Gate. To them, coming from the hot and dusty desert, it seems too beautiful for this world, with its clear streams and brilliant verdure. To a European or American, of course, it is hardly an ideal paradise, but it is nevertheless a lovely spot.

Tuesday morning I spent in the bazaars, leaving at twelve and driving as far as Chtaura, where I slept.

It was hardly daylight the next morning when I drove away from Chtaura. The sun was bright, but the air cool and sharp. Almost im-

Tower at Damascus from which St. Paul was let down in a basket.

mediately we began the ascent of the mountains, the highest point on the road being over five thousand feet in altitude. For more than two hours we travelled through fresh snow two feet deep, which had fallen the day previous. It was hard work for our three horses (which were frequently changed, both going and coming over the Damascus road),

Statue of Mehmet Ali, Alexandria.

but we got through without any mishap, arriving at the hotel at Beyrout at 12.30 P. M. At 4.30 I was taken on board the Khedivial Line steamer Rahmanieh, the same that had brought me up from Jaffa, and

General view of the Principality of Monaco.

soon afterward we sailed for Jaffa, Port Said, and Alexandria, the sea being as smooth as a lake and the weather delightful.

Our vessel spent Wednesday off Jaffa, where a number of pilgrims landed and a considerable amount of cargo was shipped. We left that place in the evening, arriving at Port Said about 8 A. M., and remained in the entrance to the Suez Canal several hours, which gave me an oppor-

Arch of Constantine, Rome.

tunity of going ashore and taking a walk. Port Said is a busy place. Nearly all the steamers passing through the canal stop there to coal, and the passengers have a chance to buy photographs, books, newspapers, etc.

Until Tuesday afternoon, March 29th, I remained quietly in Alexandria, and I then sailed in the Peninsular and Oriental steamer Hydaspes, 2,966 tons, Captain E. H. Gordon. The course was smooth and pleasant, which was fortunate, as the vessel was crowded, every available place being taken by the returning tide of pleasure-seekers from Egypt. On Friday morning, at half past nine, we were abreast

Pope Leo XIII borne in the Sedia Gestatoria

of Mount Etna, of which we had an excellent view, and soon afterward we entered the strait of Messina, which is quite narrow—three or four miles from side to side—so that we could see distinctly houses

General view of Naples.

and other objects on both shores. Beyond the city of Messina we passed the famous whirlpool Charybdis and the rock of Scylla. A Dutch cargo steamer, heavily loaded, which was proceeding ahead of us, was completely turned around by the current, and was with difficulty prevented from going ashore.

At five o'clock we were opposite the volcano of Stromboli, which is a small island at a considerable distance from the mainland, and

Restaurant at Nice.

at daylight the next morning (Saturday, April 2d) we were safely moored in the beautiful bay of Naples. I was now again on familiar ground, having made repeated visits to sunny Italy; but it is always delightful to revisit foreign spots where one knows his way about.

After passing my luggage through the customs, which was a scene of strenuous confusion and noise, and having been the victim of numerous petty annoyances and extortions, I secured a delightful room at the "West End," in a healthful location with southerly exposure, taking in the full view, over the bay, of Vesuvius, Sorrento, and Capri. I

Casino terrace, Monte Carlo.

had now completed the tour of the world, and the hard work of sightseeing for me was over, for after this I merely revisited such places as I felt would be amusing.

General view of Sorrento.

CHAPTER XIV.

FAMILIAR PLACES REVISITED.

DURING the four days of my sojourn I visited the ruins of Pompeii and Herculaneum; the splendid Museum; the Aquarium, which contains undoubtedly the finest collection of marine animals, fishes, and plants in the world; went over to Sorrento and Capri, seeing to good advantage the Blue Grotto, and ascended Mount Vesuvius.

A visit to Pompeii produces a feeling different from that which is experienced at any other of the famous places in my route. You know that all here is ancient; that the city was overwhelmed by a tremendous shower of ashes from Vesuvius more than eighteen hundred years ago, when men were living who might have witnessed the Crucifixion. You recall the great events of the early centuries of our era—the fall of the Roman Empire, the irruption of the barbarians, the career of Charlemagne; then the long night of the dark ages; the slow rise of the Russian Empire; the Norman conquest of England; then the revival of learning, and the discovery of the New World, and the wonderful story of its settlement—and then try to realize that this piece of still life, which looks like a ruin of yesterday, has quietly slept through it all, waiting for the spade of the nineteenth century simply to remove the ashes and uncover its beauties. If it looked old and moss-grown and mouldy, you could comprehend its great age. But the wheel-marks on the paving-stones look like those in Broadway, and the colours on the walls are as fresh as in the lobby of a modern hotel; and the little wine-shops, though silent and odourless, look very much like those in the older Italian cities to-day. You visit the house of

View of the Forum, Rome.

Pansa, and you see the pretty court-yard, with its little basin in the centre, and its bit of statuary, and its leaden pipes that brought water to the fountain (suggestive, where they are laid bare, of modern plumb-

House of Pansa, Pompeii.

ers' bills), and you almost expect to see the children in their play dart out from some shadowy angle of the wall.

Only a portion of the city has yet been restored to the sunlight. But a few additional rooms are opened each year by removal of the

Senate Chamber in the Luxembourg Palace, Paris.

ashes, swept clean, carefully examined, and the walls washed. In time the whole pretty town will stand forth again in the bright sunlight — unless. Look up at Vesuvius! At any moment he may repeat his performance of A. D. 79, and in a single night replace all the ashes and cinders that have been slowly carried out by the barrow-load since the excavation was begun in the middle of the last century.

On April 6th I went by rail to Rome, and had good accommodations at the Hotel Quirinale. The weather there was delightful, and I cannot express how much I enjoyed the driving each day on the Pincian

Hill, and in the grounds of the Villa Borghese, where the flower of the Roman nobility are to be seen in the afternoon in their splendid and well-appointed turnouts.

The King and Queen of Italy, both of whom I afterward met, deserve their great popularity, for two more gracious sovereigns it would be difficult to find. The Queen is the perfection of loveliness, graceful-

The Casino, Vichy.

ness, affability, and kindness. She returns the salutation of the poorest workman with the same sweet smile and cordial manner with which she acknowledges that of the richest and grandest noble; and King Humbert's kindly sovereignship can hardly be too highly praised.

I spent some time in looking through the galleries at the Vatican, the Capitol, and the Borghese Villa; and of course went to St. Peter's,

The Bourse, Paris.

St. Paul's outside the Walls, St. Maria Maggiore, the Church of St. John Lateran, the Forum, the Coliseum, and other places of interest.

St. Peter's is always enjoyable, whether one sympathizes with the religion of which it is the seat or not. As you pull aside the great leather mattress that serves for a noiseless door, and stand within, you feel as if you had entered another world — a world in which the past and the future are but one continuous existence, and the present a narrow and almost insignificant border-land between. All that one has ever read of it seems to come back like a dream. You think of

View on the Arno, Florence.

Macaulay's famous characterization of the Roman Catholic Church, in which for half a century Protestant writers have striven to find the logical flaw; and you think of Hawthorne's simple but effective descriptions in "The Marble Faun." Then you wonder which of the little confessionals it was that Miriam visited; and a thousand other fancies and memories, from the most childish to the most philosophical, run through your mind as you stroll along in the mighty nave.

Unlike St. Peter's, the Coliseum speaks only of the past — a past that was grand in its art and its power, but essentially barbaric in its humanity. The fact that the Coliseum covers nearly the same extent of ground as the Great Pyramid naturally suggests comparisons. The two are typical of the peoples that built them. The Pyramid is but a solid mass of stone, with a small chamber for a few mummies.

Place de la Concorde, Paris.

The Coliseum was built to hold eighty thousand living persons and amuse them. The great sepulchre by the Nile has stood practically unharmed for four thousand years, and may stand for fourteen thousand more; the great circus by the Tiber is but two thousand years old and is a ruin. The tomb-builder appears to be everywhere the strongest of architects.

On April 10th I left for Florence, where I remained but two days. I had a good opportunity of seeing the Florentine aristocracy each afternoon in the Cascine, that beautiful park on the banks of the Arno, and

Interior of St. Peter's, Rome.

at the Piazzale Michelangelo. I visited the Uffizi Gallery, the Pitti Palace, the Duomo and Baptistery with its "Gates of Paradise"—and the Church of Santa Croce.

If Rome is the capital of the Christian Church, Florence is the centre of Christian art. Nowhere else in the world is there such a concentration of masterpieces, though Paris, Munich, Rome, and other capitals have their priceless art treasures. Florence is one of the most beautiful cities of this peninsula, lying in the valley of the Arno, with the Apennines around it; and six centuries ago it was the richest city of Europe.

From Florence, I went to the picturesque little city of Lucca. The

Statue of Louis XIV, Place Bellecour, Lyons.

drive around its ramparts is very beautiful and interesting. In this town is the Cathedral of St. Martino, where the cross of Nicodemus, which is said to have been transferred in a miraculous manner from

Jerusalem, is preserved; the Church of St. Frediano and St. Giovanni, the latter containing the superb tomb of Nicolo Diodati; and the Palazzo Orsetti, the old home of the Diodati family, whose arms still remain, carved in stone, over the two principal entrances.

Lucca was especially interesting to me, as it was here that my ancestors, the noble line of the Diodati, originated in 1300, and achieved great

The Casino at Monte Carlo.

honour and power in the following centuries. Their title has been confirmed in France, Austria, and Italy, and inheres to all descendants, both in the male and the female line. The family is extinct in Italy, but still flourishes, as counts and countesses of the Holy Roman Empire, in Geneva in the male line, and in America in the female line.

Proceeding to Pisa, I saw the Leaning Tower, the Duomo, the Bap-

Houses of Parliament, London.

tistery, and the Campo Santo; and thence went to Genoa and saw the monument to Christopher Columbus and the wonderful Campo Santo.

The Campanile of Pisa is not the only leaning tower in the world —there are two at Bologna—but it is the most wonderful and interesting. It is a hundred and eighty feet high, and leans thirteen feet out of the perpendicular. It is a doubtful question whether the builder intended that it should lean, or whether the foundation settled unevenly, and he accepted the fact and accommodated the superstructure to it instead of beginning anew. Certainly it has proved a greater attraction for the city than if it stood upright. It is a beautiful piece of architecture, and looks remarkably fresh, considering that it is six centuries old. This is due to the fact that it is carefully kept in repair. Occasionally the visitor to Pisa will see a derrick at the top of this tower

and one or two new pillars being drawn up to replace those that have yielded to time and weather.

Leaving Genoa early in the morning, I took, along the Mediterranean, the train running parallel to the Corneci Road, stopping at Monte Carlo, Nice, and Cannes; and, after a week spent on the lovely Riviera, I proceeded to Hyères, Toulon, Marseilles (where the cold and disagreeable *mistral* was blowing), and to Lyons and Vichy; then to Paris for a week, where the weather was warm and pleasant and everything gay and attractive. My time was agreeably spent in coaching to St. Germain and Versailles, driving in the Bois de Boulogne, dining at Armenonville, Ledoyen's, Bignon's, and Voisin's, and taking a cup of delicious tea every afternoon at Columbin's in the Rue Cambon. I was sorry to leave beautiful Paris, but I had to hurry on to London, arriving just at the beginning of the season there. I remained in London ten days, and was busy shopping, but managed to find time to go coaching to Tunbridge Wells, Brighton, and St. Albans, and to have a few rides in Rotten Row.

Leaving London on May 10th, I went direct to Liverpool, *via* the London and Northwestern, the finest railway in the world, spent the night in Liverpool, and sailed on Wednesday, May 11th, at 4 P. M., by that magnificent "ocean greyhound," the Majestic, ten thousand tons, Captain H. Parsell, R. N. R. After a fairly good voyage I arrived in New York on Wednesday afternoon, May 18th, having been absent seven months and four days.

Is it needful to say how glad I was to be back again under the Stars and Stripes?—for, after all, "there is no place like home."

www.ingramcontent.com/pod-product-compliance
Lightning Source LLC
Chambersburg PA
CBHW032028220426
43664CB00006B/397